Inside

W9-ALM-364

Less 20%

19.96

Purchased by: _____

INSIDE THE VOLCANO

MY LIFE WITH
MALCOLM LOWRY

Jan Gabrial

St. Martin's Press
New York

INSIDE THE VOLCANO
Copyright © Jan Gabrial, 2000. All rights reserved. Printed in the United
States of America. No part of this book may be used or reproduced in any
manner whatsoever without written permission except in the case of brief
quotations embodied in critical articles or reviews. For information, address
St. Martin's Press, New York, N.Y. 10010

Quotations from "What the Thunder Said" and "The Love Song of J Alfred
Prufrock," on pages 67 and 171, from T.S. Eliot, *Collected Poems 1909-62*,
reproduced by permission of Faber & Faber Ltd.

Quotations from *The Waste Land,* page 67, reproduced by permission of Faber
and Faber, Ltd.

Quotations from unpublished letters of Malcolm Lowry on pages 1, 5, 6, 7,
20, 22, 31, 32, 36, 38, 63,64, 65, 66, 75, 130, 139, 140, 141, 143, 144, 160,
166, 174, 175, 177, 181, 183, 185, 189, 190, 191, and 195-97 appear here
courtesy of Sterling Lord Literistic, Inc.

Library of Congress Cataloging-in-Publication Data

Gabrial, Jan.
    Inside the volcano: my life with Malcolm Lowry / by Jan Gabrial.
        p. cm.
    Includes bibliographical references and index.
    ISBN 0-312-23277-2
    1. Lowry, Malcolm, 1909-1957—Marriage. 2. Authors, English—20th
    century—Biography. 3. Americans—Europe—Biography. 4. Authors'
    spouses—Biography.
    5. Gabrial, Jan—Marriage. I. Title.

    PR6023.O96 Z64 2000
    813'.54—dc21
    [B]   00-036909

Book design: Acme Art, Inc.
First edition: November 2000
10 9 8 7 6 5 4 3 2 1

CONTENTS

"The music I heard with you was more than music,
and the bread I broke with you was more than bread."

To my parents, Lion and Emily van der Heim,
and to fond memories of Malcolm Lowry.

Prologue

Christ, Jan, even your name is the same: the character
I invented may be clumsily done, but the girl without
whom I could not live and because of whom it seemed
I might be about to die of sheer inertia and despair from
not finding her, was yourself.

—Malcolm Lowry, after our first meeting in Spain

When I first saw Malcolm Lowry in Granada, Spain, on May 19, 1933, bells did not ring nor did rockets flash. In fact, I barely noticed him, registering merely, and peripherally at that, two solid florid men at an adjoining table, one balding, a third man, smaller, nutlike; and a pallid "madonna" whose dark hair, tightly pinned, lent her an aspect of enforced submissiveness.

The balding man unfolded a *New York Times Book Review,* revealing an article and photograph of Conrad Aiken, a likeness unmistakably his own. (The nutlike figure I later learned was Edward Burra, the painter.) The florid figure was a somewhat overweight Malcolm Lowry.

I had arrived at the Villa Carmona pension the previous night from Ronda, where I'd encountered a blond young Syrian named Calef, good company and nearly as committed a traveler as I, and had agreed to meet him shortly in Seville. I was musing on this when the madonna paused at my table to introduce herself as Clarissa Aiken and invited me to visit the gypsy caves with her. Later I'd learned that she'd been urged to do so by her husband. That evening Calef phoned me from Ronda. Impatient for reunion, he proposed joining me the next day.

The following morning, planning a visit to the Generalife Gardens of the Alhambra, I invited Mrs. Aiken (known as Jerry) to accompany me, but in her stead she offered Malcolm Lowry, a name I recognized, having admired his "Seducto Ad Absurdum" in *Best British Short Stories of 1931.* Malcolm was then 23, I, 21.

In my journal notes that day I wrote of him as "moderately tall, fine-featured, heavy of build, and possessed of a commanding presence."

Some years later, a would-be biographer produced the frisky tale that in the Generalife Malcolm had fallen on top of me while I, intent upon seduction, received instead the entire plot of his novel

Ultramarine. Intriguing though this whimsy might appear, "heavy of build" had not been idly noted. Quite slight myself, addicted to survival, and pampered by my European friends, I was never that haphazard in my availability.

On that first day I wrote, "One of the gladdest, maddest mornings of my life . . . scrambling through underbrush and filthy, and through it all laughing so much as to be practically ill . . . After lunch Malcolm avowed romantic inclinations, whether or not believable I don't know and doubt that he does either." The result was that I arrived at the station too late to greet Calef and reached the pension only to learn he'd left for his hotel. To make up for it, I took coffee with him after supper and promised to meet him the next afternoon. Then I went out with Malcolm.

"Squelched progressive tendencies on M's part with the flat statement, 'I'm not going to have an affair with you, Mr. Lowry, if that's what you mean.' It was awkwardly done, but served."

The following morning I returned to the Alhambra gardens and sat reading Malcolm's advance copy of *Ultramarine* till Malc arrived. My journal refers to him as "strangely clumsy, as in love with himself as Narcissus, savagely truthful at one moment and a gorgeous *farceur* the next." I was, I decided, "madly in love with Malcolm Lowry the author." It was not until three that I remembered Calef but by that time it was too late. Malcolm had captivated me.

My conduct so far could hardly have enchanted Calef, yet such was his ardor that when I rejoined him after supper he not only did not reproach me but proposed again.

In Paris and Berlin I'd juggled dates, three, four, and sometimes five a day, but they'd been carefree, light-hearted, undemanding. Now, drowning in ardor, exhaustion had set in. I was back at the pension by ten, praying for sleep, but Malcolm was waiting and Malcolm wanted to walk. For three more hours, then, we walked, words bubbling forth from Malc as from a stream. Parting, we pledged we'd meet in London during August. Before dropping rocklike into bed, I managed a few lines: "Why do my love affairs always come in clusters?"

What I had not then recognized was that Malcolm, during those two days, had been largely drunk, and that his inability to grasp a glass, his wildness, and his stubbornness were alcohol-induced.

At 5 A.M. I was roused by the groaning of my ancient Spanish door, and there was Malcolm, pajama-clad, rosy-looking and rested. I was neither and could have murdered him. He thrust a note toward me, sat on my bed, rolled inward, and endeavored to embrace me. Never receptive to being pawed, I fought to disengage myself from a jumble of tentacles, but abruptly Malcolm sat up looking sheepish. Premature ejaculation had taken place. My subsequent journal entry born of exasperation and fatigue proved ill chosen: "Strange how small slight men appear more favored by nature than powerful brutes like M."

That morning as planned I departed for Seville, Calef momentarily in tow though bound not for Seville but for Algeciras. I'd managed to so thoroughly discourage him with outrageous fictions of my temperament and exploits that he'd at last concurred it was best we separate. A gentle man, capable of rare tolerance and understanding, he deserved better from me. But he could not have written *Ultramarine*. He was not Malcolm Lowry.

In Aiken's fabrications in his autobiographical essay *Ushant,* Calef is a Frenchman, probably because we spoke in French, and not only did we depart in unison but likewise arrived like a matched pair from Ronda. Add to this Aiken's apparent fixation with high heels (mine in particular), frequently referring to them as "faithless" and "pitiless," and this lurid scenario was woven about poor Calef lending this apocryphal tale its ultimate titillating touch.

When Calef left the train, I reread Malcolm's 5 A.M. note: "Jan, I love you. The only time and the last time in a life full of evasions and mirrors behind mirrors . . . You are so beautiful you make me tremble, but that would happen to anybody . . . don't let (our star) fall . . . it is there and it's nobody else's and it's set and it's for us and if it fell it would be the earth going out . . ." He closed with three lines from an e.e. cummings poem and signed it, "My own sweet love . . . till August . . ."

At Seville I found more letters from Malcolm, in his tiny and distinctive script on paper torn from ever-present copybooks.

> . . . one more night and your name on my lips as forever . . . your door is still down there below . . . the stairs are soundless as slippered feet. Oh my dear, how I love you and this time the boast that no one has loved as I is true . . . No one has lived the dream of the sea, the dream of your eyes and your hair . . . I know you think I was strange and ungainly but those were only my corpse clothes . . . when you are dying of love you grow less lovely until you are merely a skull purring to the ideal of the skull; now I am alive again, launched, my noon sighted . . . I want to kiss your hair and to be yours oh most wholly and forever . . .

In a further letter he wrote that if we got together there was nothing we couldn't do. I'd not left even the scrap of a note behind but what I had left him was a lifetime. In yet another letter he wrote that during the past year he'd lost all contact with the world, ceasing to shave, to wash, to eat or exercise, lacking energy even to go to pubs . . . no wonder he'd been queer and trembling when he'd met me. "The wonder is I didn't fall down dead the first time I saw you . . ." He concluded with "the thought that you might have given to others what you would not give to me rankles with a dreadful bitter pain."

Noting that "I am really in love with Malcolm, although I don't desire him," I worried whether or not to tell him of my one love of substance, and finally forwarded a 16-page reply detailing a full account of my first romance while at dramatic school in New York. I was, however, prudent enough to omit mention of my European flings, not being, after all, in the confessional.

In further letters he wrote: "Three months, three months, three months, and to be able to kiss your hair again . . . and to be with you in London. Oh my darling, London is, I think, the most sinister city in the world, its oldness and darkness and secretness is . . . like some filthy old railway station in hell, but when you come it will blossom whitely . . . it is certainly life there when tavern doors are on the swing . . ."

We were now writing each other constantly. He quoted Baudelaire's vow to his *maitresse:* "You are more than my religion, you are my superstition," and wrote luminously of Rye, a seaport which had lost its sea, envisioning us there together in a bright glowing world of our own making.

> In loving you, I feel extraordinarily near to earth . . . life has been this dark, silent thing for me so far . . . now I'd love to work in a garden, to see things grow . . . really to create with you . . . and stand together and wonder at it. Oh Jan, I love you, but not only your loveliness . . . nor because it was Spring and there was a Spring in your heart more than heart could bear, nor because I knew we could be happy . . . I love you for your whole self . . . because I see into you and I see there a bright world of our own making . . . "Christ that my love were in my arms and I in my bed again!"

❧   ❧   ❧

Had we been older, less dazzled by each other, the obstacles confronting us might have suggested pause, for Malcolm was beguiled by amulets and charms while I, so newly released from a prolonged dormancy, tiptoed around the fragile fields of hedonism.

But always his own protagonist, Malcolm envisioned me as his personal creation. "Christ, Jan, even your name is the same: the character I invented may be clumsily done, but the girl without whom I could not live . . . was yourself!" But I wasn't his invention, and stubbornly protective of my new-found selfhood, reluctant to be absorbed, I warned him that he must accept me as the girl I was. And indeed, with the passing months affording us first comfort in our roles and then delight, such differences slowly ceased—or seemed to cease—to matter.

Curtain Raiser

Life's overture has just been performed.
The curtain rises. The play is to begin.
Act your part the way I expect you to act,
and all will be well.

—Lion van der Heim, my father, in 1923,
on my graduation from grammar school,
only a few months before his death

As Malcolm mourned his lack of early love, I mourned my father, dead at fifty, a musical prodigy born in Rotterdam who, at the age of twelve, had won a scholarship from Queen Wilhelmina to Brussels Conservatory. Arriving in America in his early 20s, he was already a brilliant violinist, proficient in five instruments and fluent in half a dozen languages. When, in the flood of reminiscences that succeeded Malcolm's death, I found my father referred to by a witless churl as "probably a bootlegger" I was homicidal.

Mother, small, feisty, and good looking, began teaching in her teens and never stopped, her dedication warmed by her affection for small children. Reading aloud to me from the time I was a baby, father and she together sparked my lifelong love of literature.

At four, I started school, in Kate Greenaway bloomer dresses and fat ribboned pigtails, both of which I hated. By the time I graduated from high school at 15, swamped in a sea of leggy blondes—for I was always youngest and smallest in my classes—I had determined to escape from academia; instead of Radcliffe, for which mother had been hoping, I enrolled at the American Academy of Dramatic Arts. While there I had my first real date, with a whimsical young writer—Fran Mattison. To my amazement, he fell in love with me.

After summer stock (where I first took the stage name of Jan Gabrial) and modest roles in the theater plus a fruitless stint as Lee Patrick's understudy (she missed nary a performance), I was cast as the ingenue lead in a vaudeville skit erroneously intended to be a comedy. My vis-à-vis was Teddy Gordon, who bore a startling resemblance to the blond, young, and still idolized Prince of Wales. Ted shared the opulent digs of Eldon, a waspish writer of simmering religious novels, weighty with sin and regeneration and much purple prose. This household was swelled from time to time by Anne Hunt, whose liaison

with Ted had waxed and waned for years. I was convinced sophistica-
tion could scale no greater heights than this ménage.

Between engagements in upstate New York towns like Watervliet
and Saugerties, though we likewise appeared (more grandly) in Albany
and Troy, Ted and I haunted booking offices and foraged for fabric
remnants for my costumes. (Ted was a skilled designer and Anne's
clothes were stunning.)

We hear much of the liberating sexual revolution of the sixties, but
that of the Roaring Twenties was no less dramatic. "Companionate
marriage" might be denounced from pulpits but the arts bristled with
relaxed moral codes, defying Billy Sunday's thunderings of hellfire. I
recall with delight the amused veneration accorded *Les Grandes horizon-
tales* in the so-called Naughty Nineties in my wise, beloved France.

At about this time I read Stendhal's *Lamiel,* with its famous scene
in which Lamiel pays the cloddish Jean Breville to seduce her. "What?"
she asks herself, "can love be merely this? What's the use of prohibiting
it so violently?" And she bursts into laughter as she repeats, "What, this
love they all talk about, is that all there is to it?" "Is that all," which
Edward Rod called the leitmotif of Stendhal's life. Like Lamiel, I was
eager to investigate for myself. My theatrical and literary heroines—
Bernhardt, Duse, Rachel, George Sand, and Colette—had each led
spectacularly experimental lives. My own, alas, had so far been unsul-
lied. What if I died a virgin? Lord knows the possibilities looked bleak
enough. Fran was usually upstate. The only man whom I saw regularly
was Teddy, whose romantic ties were surely more than ample. Besides,
how on earth could I approach the subject? "Take me?" He'd have
choked with laughter!

But he didn't. Two days before my seventeenth birthday, with
Eldon out of town, we were alone in the apartment. It was—alas—as
well that I'd read *Lamiel,* for hopeless as Jean Berville had proved to
be, he might well have outpointed Ted. We ploughed through l'amour
in a state of casual good fellowship (though I was sure I was fatally in
love), and finally, with some measure of relief, abandoned it. Happily,
the good fellowship survived. While I'd failed to experience the oft-

sung joys of sex, I'd at least learned to create a fetching wardrobe. It was not a total loss. In fact, Teddy and Anne and I now became comrades, and presently Fran came back into my life.

In January 1931, an event occurred that was to change my world: Mother had been tutoring the obnoxious son of a vapid pretty woman named Helen who was convinced that her dentist was madly, if secretly, in love with her and that only her own divorce could effectuate their union. Reno-bound to attempt to force his hand, she invited me along for company, and flying merrily in the face of superstition we left New York on the thirteenth and headed south. By Thursday we had gotten as far as Appalachia, by which time it had become apparent that Helen was addicted not only to her dentist but likewise to White Lightning. At Knoxville, where we passed our second night, she secured a bottle of the harsh corn liquor and nipped happily away at it throughout the next day's drive.

Snow had covered the Tennessee mountain roads with solid ice by the time we approached Surgoinsville—and then it happened! Swerving to escape a large oncoming truck and at the same time avoid the precipice, Helen overcorrected and crashed into the truck broadside. Those being pre-safety-glass days, when I slammed into the windshield, it shattered and so did my nose.

I could remember my name but absolutely nothing else. When I finally reassembled pieces of my memory I found myself in a primitive drafty cabin with neither heat nor electricity, my abortive theatrical career as shattered as my face. Through two subsequent surgeries and the artistry of Dr. J. Eastman Sheehan, I emerged from my nightmare feeling, for the first time in my nearly twenty years, that I was pretty. And now life rearranged itself.

Back in New York, while still at Doctor's Hospital (where I spent ten days), I read a joyous article by William Lyons Phelps about a cycling trip through England and the lights came on. My new face and modeling millinery provided the ticket of my dreams . . . a one-way passage from New York to France. In any case, by that time I had decided that I might follow my second bent, which was writing.

On April 6, 1932, I sailed on the SS *American Importer* with a suitcase of clothes I'd made myself and the book which would become my Bible for the next two years, *Through Europe on Two Dollars a Day.* Mother gave me her blessing. "I know you've done things of which I wouldn't approve," she told me staunchly, "but so long as I don't know about them it's all right." It was her absolution to her cub, releasing me. She was a gallant lady and my friend through life.

Of the golden cities of Europe, I have seen many. Cherbourg, where the ship finally put in after our Atlantic crossing, was least among them. It rose from the pages of Julian Green, squat, bitterly cold, streaming with rain, blackish-gray. I settled at a cheap hotel and fled the livid wallpaper and fleshy-looking bed to explore the town where I'd be immured till the 6 A.M. Paris train. Wandering streets of soiled cafes and ugly shops, I hurried till I reached the city's outskirts. Low white cottages, vivid roofs, ubiquitous shutters, and forbidding walls. "The Closed Garden" indeed.

Having eschewed dinner as a gesture toward economy, I settled for black coffee and a cigarette in a waterfront cafe which announced *En-lish -pok-n* in a corner of its windowed entry. It proved an inauspicious choice. "Cafe noir," got me exactly nowhere until I made vague motions to indicate a cup.

"*Ah, oui . . .*" the waitress exclaimed happily. "*Café natur! Tres bien, Mademoiselle.*" Three men at a nearby table snickered. I lit a cigarette to appear world-wise. Seven French grammars and not one of them contained *café natur!* The waitress brought a small cup with a thick black bitter liquid which repaid me later with a panic attack. Trouble began anew when she reappeared.

"*Combien ça fait?*" I asked her doubtfully.

"*Soixante-quinze, Mademoiselle.*"

Every word I had faithfully studied had gone south, but she was quite patient with me. A small gold coin (which resembled mother's dollar gold-piece) proved insufficient, but from a five-franc note she returned change. My *café natur,* it seemed, had cost three cents. Back in the noisome hotel room, two people next door making vociferous love all night in groaning French did nothing to allay my feelings of abandonment.

But the "Umbrellas of Cherbourg" receded forever as I sallied forth next day into the brilliant Paris sunshine. Most large cities can, in time, *become* friendly, but Paris *is* if only you are receptive to her loveliness.

Here, like a litany, I sang to myself that I was at last in the city where Balzac (mourning each orgasm as the loss of another book), envisioned his *Comédie Humaine;* where students unhitched the horses from the carriage of the very young Sidonie-Gabrielle Colette to pull it through the Paris streets in homage; where my beloved Stendhal paid his way into society with his conversation; where Chopin and Sandeau and deMusset, among the lovers of the fabulous George Sand, helped to enlarge her legend. With the sun setting over the Place de la Concorde, I breathed what will always be, for me, the scent of Paris—a compilation of hot, musty subway odors overlaid with garlic and with perfumes and with wine. If I were to name one day of perfect happiness, it would have to have been that.

"Were I to die tomorrow," I wrote, "it would all have been worthwhile. I am in Paris!"

After my first week at the Hotel Regina (where I'd negotiated a pretty room . . . no bath . . . for a dollar a night . . . more than I could afford for long)—I moved into Mon Foyer, a pension run by Mme. Goifon and her sons at 8 Square Delormel. Madame accepted me into her household with but four stipulations: that I pay my bills in advance; speak French at table; not forget my key and thereby wake up the establishment; and refrain from the seduction of her sons, who were of such unfortunate ugliness that I all but took an oath. With demi-pension the monthly tab equaled $37.50, well within my budget, and the room was pleasant. Among the residents was a beautiful Hungarian, two years my senior. Taking her baccalaureate at the Sorbonne, she spoke five languages and radiated an infectious gaiety. Her name was Erszi and we became inseparable.

In Paris I caught up with my belated adolescence and found myself immersed in comradeship and romance. To be young and pretty and light-hearted and American in Paris in 1932 was to possess the world.

On June 11, I turned 21. With Erszi and her friends we picnicked near Fontainebleau, and that night descended on the Hôpital Salpêtrière for a ribald supper with the students of pharmacy. Dining room walls sported explicit and merrily pornographic murals and the songs we sang were bawdy, yet the evening brimmed with an exuberance that banished smarminess. It was a bang-up fête.

On the twenty-sixth I left for Heidelberg after a farewell evening with Erszi and our friends. In a scant ten weeks she'd become the sister I had never had, and in leaving Paris I would miss her most.

I was later to learn that this gorgeous, laughing, generous-hearted girl was to die horribly with all but one of her elegant and cultured family in that abomination known to the world as Auschwitz.

Act One

On January 4, 1933, I left Berlin where I'd been part of the frenetic gaiety mirrored by Christopher Isherwood in his Berlin stories. I'd spend three *fabelhaft* months blithely skirting the fringes of history, for these were the weeks just prior to Hitler's *Putsch*. Assured by my Berliner friends that Hitler was an aberration (for the prevailing fear was always of the communists), we danced at Resi and the Hotel Adlon, *bummelled* at *kaffeehausen* and Haus Vaterland, fell in and out of love, and joined Berliners in Cloud Cuckooland.

From March through much of May that spring I explored Tunisia and Algeria, their oases, and the glorious old cities of Morocco. North Africa fascinated me more than any place I'd visited save only Paris.

In one of my accumulating journals I noted: "Travel replaces words and names with pictures. Veiled women and turbaned men and at dusk the wailing summons of the muezzin; slow, undulating camels outside the great walls of holy Kairouan, while within, the savage séance of the Aissaouas, who hammer swords into and through their tongues and noses and cheeks and all parts of their bodies, drawing no blood; the naked dancers in Casablanca's City of Prostitutes; the high bright voices of the bride's attendants at the desert wedding outside Nefta, while the bride herself, adorned with gold, awaited her bridegroom, veiled and motionless, her palms stained with henna; then Marrakech, legendary, brick red, abloom with gardens, boasting the vastness of the Djema El Fna where a snake charmer wound a cobra round my ankle; and the day in Fez I spent inside a harem among the loveliest women I had ever seen. On go the pictures and the memories, as tumbling and as irreplaceable as these days of my youth which memory, at least, perpetuates."

On the boat from Tangier to Gibraltar I encountered an Englishman whose heartiness was somewhat overwhelming. Once ashore he stood me breakfast at the Cafe Royal where we met with a Hungarian

who offered me a job with his small troupe—his wife and two girls only—
assuring me I'd learn the dance routines within a week. I might have
considered it for a month or two—one more experience—but he
demanded a six months' contract so I passed it up, thereby ensuring my
first meeting with Malcolm, only four days distant in Spain. And all that
thereon followed.

∽ ∽ ∽

In Marseilles (after my departure from Spain) as always on my travels,
there were letters waiting at the American Express, and at a port-side
cafe, rich with the smells of the sea, I read and reread Malcolm's. Its
tone mirrored his mood, gray, rain induced and somber. He wrote he
was drinking tea, which he detested, "because for the present I am not
allowed to drink anything else . . . oh hell, Jan . . . And you in
Marseilles." Where did I walk? With whom did I speak? "Are the
skeletons of ships in the harbor dark? And what do these worlds of iron
conceal?" Did eternal lovers still climb stairs, eternal mariners reel back
to everlasting ships and eternal deserters retreat into shadows? "I can
say only the tritest things to you I know, but when I say that I love you
I know that my message speeds through space. Windblown shepherds
pause at their work; swaying steeplejacks pause; the stoker leans on his
slicebar: 'What has passed this way?'"

One of travel's brightest aspects comes with revisiting places you
have loved. Paris would always head my list, but Florence would be
close. Just driving again through its familiar streets brought contentment and anticipation.

The Pension Annalese was a rendezvous for creative artists. As on
my visit earlier in the tour, there was an amusing crowd including Harry,
an architect, and Gardner, an artist on a scholarship and blessed with
an impish grin. Again, in Florence there were letters from Malcolm and
also from friends in Heidelberg, Paris, Berlin, and Budapest. I opened
Malcolm's first. This one, however, deposited an unwonted load of
guilt. Even its tenor sounded foreign: "*You don't have to understand if*

you don't wish to but I can't fling about nearly as carelessly and thoughtlessly as you do from one place to another . . ."

Fling about? Thoughtlessly? Strange words to the ideal nymph errant, as he had called me in Granada, who had previously been considered tarnish-proof.

I did not yet recognize the indication that all would not remain perpetual bliss in Eden, so I again tried to explain why my arrival in England might be delayed a week; the date for our reunion had never been engraved on the white cliffs of Dover. We had known one another a bare two days and now, to my discomfort, I discovered I was writing him defensively.

On my last night in Florence, Gardner and I went for a farewell coffee. There were questions in my mind about Malcolm's sobriety, and since Gardner and I were enormously attracted to one another, we planned a tour of the French chateau country, though this would not interfere with my other sketched-in stopovers in Europe. Returning to the pension, we encountered a tribe of knickered, booted, and knapsacked Nazi *jungen* belting out *Deutschland Uber Alles*. It went well with my resurgent dysentery.

From Paris, where Gardner rejoined me, we left on our bicycle trip through the chateau country. For a committed wanderer like myself, it would have been unthinkable to leave France without this pilgrimage. Altogether we visited a dozen castles.

The termination of our trip was thorny. At the bicycle shop where all had been joviality, the *commerçant* refused to credit Gardner the 60 francs he had spent on bicycle repairs. After much arguing from me, for Gardner spoke little French, he did agree to refund 20 francs, but at this sum Gardner balked. I rashly renewed the argument, at which point the *commerçant* lost his cool and howled at us, snatching the money he had handed to Gardner and now refusing even our hundred-franc deposits. With everyone screaming at once I shouted at him to at least return these and we'd leave, whereupon he threw me bodily into the street, leaving Gardner inside still arguing.

"What did you do, grow roots?" I snapped at Gardner when he rejoined me. But, where I'd failed, he had retrieved our money.

∽   ∽   ∽

In his cramped, distinctive script, Malc wrote that *Ultramarine* had received a rave review, even labeling it "great." A further letter placed him in London, attempting to find a home for his play, adapted from Nordahl Grieg's *The Ship Sails On.* And *Story* had accepted "On Board the West Hardaway."

And finally a longer letter which disturbed me, not for its words so much as for its tone, for he now instructed me to bypass London and meet him instead in Plymouth. It would, he admitted, be more costly, but I should sail only on the *Paris,* which boasted a glass dance floor, miniature golf, a rifle range, even a Punch and Judy show. Since he offered no reason for a change of plans and we'd agreed all along to reunite in London, that still seemed to be the wisest choice. And so I wrote. From him, I next received a cool, offended letter, though laced with a grudging soupçon of relief. He'd wrecked his short-lived M.G. Magna, but was fortunately unhurt. Thank God I had not been with him when he crashed! Oddly enough, although the car was totaled, for some months he referred to it as viable: "When we go to the South of France we must take the MG," for example. But he was clearly quite put out that I'd not arrive in Plymouth.

This letter, like its predecessor, struck a note so at variance with Malcolm's constant declarations of amour that I was decidedly deflated. I had failed to accede to a seemingly frivolous demand; now he was sulking. Could it be that enchanted as he was with words—their sounds, their colors, their powers to manipulate—what he'd evoked through them was only writing-paper love?

Any further exhilaration was further dampened when, as foreshadowed, Malcolm not only failed to meet the channel ferry but even to return to London.

I checked my bags, bought an Atlas Guide, and set out to locate the Chelsea boarding house recommended by Reggie, an Englishman whom I'd met at the Prado in Madrid. To my pleased surprise, he appeared while I was arranging for a room, and we dined together. Though he

guided me ably through Piccadilly and the West End, there seemed
something infinitely depressing about the city, as though I'd returned
home prematurely, and I felt homesick for the friends I'd made in Paris.

I left a note for Malc at the Astoria, a somewhat seedy hotel in Soho
and his favorite hangout in the city. My note produced no results, nor
was there word from him at the American Express. After the months of
passionate avowals, I was increasingly deflated. "Damn the man anyhow," I wrote, and repeated "What kind of writing-paper lover *is* he?"

So I took bus rides, lunched at a pub, visited the Tate and Wallace
Galleries—and it rained. Reggie and I caught *The Late Christopher
Bean* at the St. James, and it rained. We went to Richmond and took a
steam launch to Hampton Court. It still rained and I developed a cold
and seriously contemplated a return to Paris.

Then, on my fourth day in London, while I was poring over a
lovesick note from Gardner, Malcolm appeared at the American
Express and contended, not too convincingly, that we'd managed to
miss each other not only at Victoria Station but also, and repeatedly, at
the American Express. I summed up our reunion and the subsequent
weeks in my journal:

> Malc is less striking than I'd remembered and our entertainment took
> the form of dashing frenziedly from pub to pub. Only at my insistence
> did we have a so-so lunch before recommencing the pub crawl. Harry
> arrived from Paris this morning and we'd arranged a date for tonight,
> but Malcolm so absolutely forbade it that to save trouble I gave in and
> canceled Harry. Actually, with him I'd have spent a far more plea-
> surable evening.
>
> Malcolm and I simply wandered about until I grew tired and
> snappy, and we began to quarrel. His is a strong and dominating
> nature, egotistical as Cain, and while he claims to love me, he wills
> always to be the *master*. I am readily led, but to push or force me
> rouses every whisker of resistance; the feet come down flat and I balk.
>
> He has asked me to marry him, but smothered as I feel, I'm
> dubious.

Tuesday, September 26

Harry phoned and I agreed to meet him at 10:30 at the British Museum. I had barely hung up when Malcolm called to announce we were flying to Wales this afternoon and to meet him at 12:30. It was less an invitation than a Royal Command, but since I've never flown, I acquiesced.

It was great to see Harry, who looked rather lonely. Jabbering nonstop, we wandered through the museum, reminiscing about Florence and Gardner and Paris. At 12:30, I met Malc and we collected Tom Forman who will be our pilot. Wales has been postponed until tomorrow, but because today was glorious, we flew instead to Reading, stopping at several airports for cocktails and for brandy. Though the plane was very tiny, flying is a marvelous sensation, especially the takeoffs and since we were all quite tight I have no clear memories of our return.

Back in my room, Malc and I harangued about love and marriage till past midnight by which time I was so agonizingly weary I could do nothing but send him out into the night as demanding and obstinate as a child.

Wednesday, September 27

Tom called several times this morning, terribly worried about Malc: no one knew where he was. His apprehension was contagious. It was a distinct relief when Malc turned up, almost an hour late, having— he claimed—spent the night with his taxi driver.

The weather was now foggy enough to cut, and at the Heston airport it had started drizzling. I sat around stupidly while Tom and M. made trial tests and, after consulting everything but their horoscopes, decided to postpone the flight yet again. Instead, we flew to a nearby airport for an alcoholic "tea."

Tom has left his dog in my care, a fine black spaniel who is broken-hearted. He stares at me mournfully, convinced of desertion. Malc and I argued some more tonight, but I was too wiped out to stand it and in desperation announced that our romance, such as it was, had been an obvious mistake, and asked him to please leave.

He has incredible vitality. Unfortunately, desiring me as he does, he is so unbearably insistent that all he rouses in me is exhaustion.

By morning, though my outlook had brightened, the weather looked hopeless, and Tom called to say he absolutely had to get the rented plane back today. Malcolm turned up as I was leaving for the American Express and accompanied me, leaving the sad-eyed spaniel in the room.

Two letters from Gardner, who has arranged to sail from Southampton rather than Cherbourg so that we could spend several days together. At this point, I did not know what to do. There was no time to head him off in Paris, and Malcolm and Gardner was a not-to-be-thought-of combination. On the other hand, the prospect of seeing G. again, after all the *sturm und drang* with Malcolm, would be a blessed relief.

As it happened, matters were decided for me. When he emerged from the American Express the sun was doing its best to shine, and Malcolm—mercurial as ever—was in a frenzy of optimism. So, feeling like the faithless Mildred in *Of Human Bondage,* I left a note for Gardner that I was on my way to Wales, and tried not to reflect on the wisdom of the impulse.

Back in my room, Malc played his uke and sang. Tom had not yet showed up and the dog looked ready to collapse. Suddenly the door burst open to admit Mrs. Gurney, my outraged landlady— furious at Malcolm's "unbounded impudence" at playing the ukulele in her house, and my "colossal cheek" in keeping a dog in my room all night. She would have no more of me. Embarrassed for Reggie, who had recommended me, I packed, and as soon as Tom arrived, we departed with a sorry attempt at dignity.

There was just time for a pick-me-up at Hounslow, the Heston airport, and we were off. The first hour was terribly rough going and I was sure we'd crash, yet my attitude was fatalistic . . . my primary fear that of being disabled. The fog thickened and Tom searched for some place to set down. We swooped and soared and rocked and skimmed at awkward angles, yet found no landing field. Finally we smacked down on a race course, got our bearings, took off once more, and landed at Castle Bromwich airport outside Birmingham. Here we had tea, learned of a plane which had crashed a little earlier at Hooten, our destination, and finally, towards 15:10, took off again.

A cold rain set in, and then a pea-souper. Going was awful. There was no visibility above 100 feet, and when the fog fell in grim earnest we were totally immersed. We flew, blanketed, for perhaps two minutes more, before Tom circled and landed, rather nicely, and announced it would be impossible to make Liverpool that night.

Halting a solitary motorist, whose accent was strange and puckery, we were returned to Castle Bromwich airport. When Tom had attended to the plane, we went into Birmingham, a grubby place with an ugly hotel in which I feel marooned. Chatted briefly with Tom who said Malc needs sympathy and understanding and only drinks because he has been sexually starved. To complete the pleasures of the day, the steak-and-kidney pie at dinner disagreed with me violently. What the hell am I doing in Birmingham?

Friday, September 29
The fog was still impossible this morning, thick and yellow, with a musty odor and a clammy feel. Martin Case, a friend of Malc's, dropped by and we went to a pub where he played [piano] for us. I liked him from the start.

We took off again toward three and made Hooten airport without further mishap. When we arrived, M. and I began to quarrel . . . it was a misery time. Even before we had left the airport Malc had started to drink in earnest and when the car arrived to take us to Portmeirion—nearly a four-hour drive—he was alternately loquacious and ugly and maudlin and driveling.

The hotel is lovely. Everything else is *merde*.

Saturday, September 30

Things seemed better this morning.

M. and I took a short walk, then I wrote letters. During the afternoon we visited some of his friends, where he played his uke and finished off their whisky.

When we got back to the hotel, the friendliness had vanished and I felt awkward besides because everyone here dresses for dinner and, on Malc's recommendation, I had left my good clothes in London, bringing only a few sports things, about as suitable here as was my wool suit in the Sahara.

On top of this, Malc grew tight and abusive and I wanted to wire Gardner to please come after all. We had a terrible row after supper and I very nearly left for London; only one thing stopped me: like it or not, for nearly four months, we've been writing romantic letters, presumably honestly meant and honestly believed. So, disillusioned though I unquestionably am, I feel bound to give us every chance while in England.

In spite of these nobly befuddled sentiments, by the time we reach the Gorphwysfa Hotel at Pen-y-Pas (which, by the way—in surroundings remote and stern—could have served as the setting for the *House of Usher*), M. was both noisy and belligerent. I find him impossible when drunk, totally unlike anyone I've ever known. Even his appearance changes radically. His face swells and becomes beet-red; his eyes all but disappear; his mouth works; even his sailor's gait turns into travesty.

Our hotel accommodations are primitive and damned cold. (I had my chance in Portmeirion. Have I taken the wrong turning?")

Sunday, October 1

Today broke beautifully and while I was pondering on how I could effect an at least temporary reconciliation with Malcolm—necessary if we are to be thrown so constantly together here—he came into my room smiling and looking as though he'd never been tight in his life. His recoveries from binges are miraculous. We went to breakfast as at peace with the world and each other, as though last night had never been, followed by a stroll along the Pig Track which leads to Snowdon.

In the afternoon Malcolm and Tom went for an honest-to-goodness attempt at rock-climbing, ropes, spiked shoes, et al. I did some work on Tom's typewriter, which will prove a godsend in the days ahead.

Malcolm and I talked about short stories this morning and may collaborate this winter. Evening was spent around the fireplace, reading and chatting till the debauching hour of 9:30 when I gave in to sleep and left.

At this point I was mostly writing travel notes and received neither encouragement nor distraction from Malcolm. However, when we settled for a time at Portmeirion Malc played a more positive role in discussing what I was writing.

Monday, October 2 through Sunday, October 15
The last two weeks passed, on the whole, quite well. Malc has helped a lot with my Tarragon story, and suggested a title: "Sweets to the Sweet Farewell" . . . (does Hamlet say this to the dead Ophelia?)

We lived quietly—reading, working, till one ominous quarrel marred our relations. It occurred at the halfway point. Malc had received word that his father would be driving out from Liverpool to discuss finances.

Panicking at the thought his father might discover me, he decided I must go to Carnarvon for the day. The mere idea infuriated me: I am not, after all, Malc's doxy, and there *were* three of us. To top it, when the day broke, it was pouring, and since I had both the curse and cramps, I absolutely refused to plunge into the storm for anyone.

So I remained in bed trying to read, and caught a miserable cold in the refrigerated room. As for Malcolm, the inconsiderate punk never thought to send up lunch or a snack or even some hot tea. When his father finally left, it was past 5:30 and I was seeing red.

I charged downstairs and drank two double whiskies, one after the other, to thaw out, and then told Malcolm exactly what I thought of him. This blossomed into a royal dispute, but in a day or two the atmosphere had cleared and once again we became amicable.

On October 11 Tom left for Portmeirion to meet with Bertrand Russell, and Malcolm and I, with the Gorphwysfa to ourselves, at last caught up with our reunion.

Sober, Malcolm is funny, gentle, appealing, vulnerable, and dazzling by turns. At such times he is a spellbinder. He has the sea-blue, sea-gazing Norseman's eyes; his voice is glorious; and sober or drunk, his exuberance is unflagging. In spite of our frequent battles, I am once again falling in love with him.

During my stay in Wales, I wrote mother requesting the October issue of *Story*. In my letter, I added:

Malcolm and I alternately agree beautifully and quarrel intensely. He's jealous of the friends I've made in my travels, women as well as men, and I don't suppose I shall ever conform to his idea of femininity, apparently adherent to the credo that woman was created to be meekly forever a forbearing helpmate: PERIOD! Not that I'd not be eager to aid and encourage as much as possible but to be only a voiceless shadow was never in my stars. I am not, thank God, one of the Arab women I saw often in North Africa, trudging silently not only behind her husband but behind his camels, too.

Malcolm is brilliant and will be among the greatest of British authors, but he can be selfish, sentimental, possessive and opinionated. (Come to think of it, though neither sentimental nor possessive, I am often opinionated, and frequently selfish too.) And so we quarrel and often.

In her reply, mother wrote:

Marriage isn't just a contract; it is infinitely more; it is comradeship, freedom of spirit, of mind, for both partners. "Obey" isn't in the contract because that word alone eliminates freedom for the woman. When you marry, you will suit your own heart, no one else's, and will stand on your own feet for better or worse. Mine was better, but I loved too much. I was a woman of the old school. I married a man ultramodern. There lay the difference: I saw things my way and refused to see things Lion's way . . . (blame the subconscious Germanic strain . . .)

Now I want to ask you candidly: Does M. drink to excess? If so, don't have him for anything in the world. It doesn't improve under the stress of marriage my dear . . . You are my daughter, and you have had many advantages . . . if Malcolm is worthy of you, he will be like my own child and blood but he must be worthy . . . You can afford to wait, but not too long, for life flies . . . and there are many opportunities open to you . . .

With mother in touch I never felt isolated, and, except on sexual matters, open communication was possible for which I was very grateful to her.

Monday through Friday, October 16 through 20
Had decided to go to Dublin today—Malcolm is leaving for Liverpool—but when I waked, it was pouring and cold, and I felt readier to tackle London in the rain than Dublin . . .

A broken-up and breaking-up letter from Gardner who, from the two blithe and thoughtless notes I sent from airports, deduced that he was "just another cog" in my wheel of life, and told me I had destroyed his faith in womankind. I did not know how to answer, so postponed it . . .

To the National Gallery—superb—to me second only to the Prado and Rijksmuseum. When it closed, I wandered along to the

Tower of London and the Tower Bridge, a beauty, especially with the fog drifting low across the Thames. At moments like this, London's misty loveliness can break your heart. Seven months ago on the Florence-Rome express, a Hungarian recommended the small Florina at 63 Kensington Gardens Square. It proved exactly what I wanted.

At Amexco, found a wire from Malc: "Coming through on a big choo-choo" and sure enough, at 9 P.M., the phone rang. We met outside the Dominion Theatre but from then on it was all downhill. For starters, we were never alone, picking up clutches of his friends at the Plough, going on to an artsy-fartsy party I thought stupid, and climaxing the evening with a round of bottle clubs.

Next morning with a prince of a *katzenjammer*, I vaguely recalled having made a 10 A.M. date with M., but for the life of me couldn't remember where. After a fruitless hour spent trying to reach him by phone, I dressed and dashed to the Astoria to learn he had only just rolled in and was in bed. He was still drunk of course and really looked revolting. I suggested we meet for supper at 7:30 at the Dominion and went home for a further stab at sleep.

By 7:30 it had turned into the usual cold and rainy London night and there was zero sign of Malc. Ditto at 7:45. Ditto again at 8:00. He turned up 45 minutes late, still bloated and still drunk, to be confronted by a cold, shivering lady who had built up a classic head of steam. John Sommerfield, the writer, hovered in his wake, so I tried hard to control my temper, but it was no go. After half an hour, I abandoned them in a pub and stormed home, dinnerless, lonely, and depressed.

Now finally I was able to write to Gardner, with whom these damnable denouements had never once occurred. Tom had been right in dubbing Malcolm a souse; if anything, that was an under-statement. Yet when he called me the next morning, such was the hold of his genius and magnetism that I agreed to meet him later in the day.

This time, his companion, also of Cambridge, was James Travers, who owned a bright red Riley. Malc, who could be extremely caustic, later insisted the car was the most interesting thing about him but I found him fun. After the apparently mandatory pub crawl, we drove to Sommerfield's for tea. Malc brought a bottle of whisky but no one else saw any of it. Ultimately he passed out and had to be deposited in the bedroom.

After supper Travers suggested a drink at the Marquis of Granby and who should turn up to greet us there but Malcolm! This really pulled things taut all around. Following a further round of pubs, we went out to Anna Wickham's—the poet of "Not a Pot in my Whole House is Clean." There, Malcolm and I quarreled bitterly, finally calling it quits "for good and all" in Anna's kitchen, where, by the way, not a pot that evening was.

I don't know that it's really final—our quarrels never seem to be—but candidly I'd be relieved if they were.

I wrote despondently: "M. has been on one continuous blind since he landed in London. Inescapable, the bond between him and Anna; he is greatly influenced by others without realizing it; his friends want to possess him and seem jealous of each other."

He phoned next morning but I told Dorothy, a maid at the hotel, to say I was out. At suppertime, he called again. I was still "out." He left a number for me to call but I ignored it. Physically and emotionally exhausted, I had to think things through. Drinking accompanied by dancing and fun, as in Berlin, was one thing; drinking for the unalloyed sake of drinking and solely to get drunk—that I could not even begin to understand.

To see whether I could do it, I walked over to Trafalgar Square and back, and on my return found a note from Malc: "I long for you. But remember, il faut tuer beaucoup d'amour pour arriver à l'amour." He signed it "Nigger," his Cambridge nickname.

That night I went alone to the Old Vic to see *The Cherry Orchard*. Exiting from the theater, I encountered a deluge in full force; to snag a taxi was like trying to flag down the Ark. But whom should I spot peering anxiously about but Malcolm, in a new blue mac and scarf and looking—Hallelujah—sober and excited. It was no time for dignity. With unabashed relief, I greeted both him and the taxi he had waiting.

"It proved a lovely night," I wrote in my journal. "We went to the Corner House for tea, the Cheshire Cheese for punch, and for supper to Ye Olde Cock Inn. Though I tried hard not to show it, I was absolutely delighted to see him . . . Neither of us wants to let the other go and we are miserable apart."

Sunday, October 29

At 2:30. Malc came by [the Florina] and we were nearly asphyxiated by the gas heater, which is faulty. He is arousing me more readily. Later we had supper with Hugh Sykes Davies and Betty May, the famous "Tiger Woman." She was a favorite model of Jacob Epstein's and is said to have known everyone, even Ernest Dowson and Oscar Wilde, though this seems impossible. But she is fascinating, warm, friendly, and very very attractive, as well as a wizard cook. We are invited back for dinner tomorrow together with an ex-lover of hers, Edgell Rickword. I wish Malcolm could be as relaxed as Hugh about these overlapping relationships.

What with this *stimmung*, good food, good wine, and good conversation, Malc and I somehow became engaged. I think we are both a little startled and surprised. And tentative.

Tuesday, October 31

Malc has been called to Leicester to meet with his father and Tom. This A.M. I saw him off at St. Pancras, a strange barn of a place framed in Rathaus gothic. While waiting for his train, we had tea and seemed actually to reach a deeper understanding. He has determined that I should fall in love with him, and I *am* happiest when all is well with us, but also at my most miserable during our wretched altercations.

A cable tonight from Gardner: "Forgive me. G."

If only Malc and I could find the hominess, the ease and contentment that Gardner and I knew.

Spent the evening rereading the first two chapters of *Ultramarine,* which are so vividly done they approach genius. Indeed, Malcolm's talent excuses many of his excesses; he is bound to become a noted writer because writing to him is actually a *calling.* His work is his religion; all else will remain secondary—and should.

I guess I now realized that through insecurities and through his own uncertainties about his manhood, he had this need to feel in control and to feel he was the dominant figure in our relationship.

On November 3, he returned. He was now staying with Hugh Sykes Davies and Betty May. He told me they'd enlisted him as caretaker, though who was to care for whom may well have been the matter under discussion in Leicester. At any rate, Betty and Hugh had planned a few days in Cambridge, and the place was ours. "We spent the first evening quietly," I recorded later: "supper, then Coward's *Cavalcade.* The next day we caught Pudovkin's *Deserter* and were en route to a pub when joined by Sommerfield. With no warning, Malc turned difficult, bade John a rude good night, and left him standing in the street, which provoked another of our quarrels till, in a still further *volte face,* he recounted his adaptation of *The Ship Sails On* (on which, incidentally, he is collaborating with Sommerfield). The play may or may not be good . . . I can't decide from the recital . . . but I think not; it isn't up to *Ultramarine* and is too similar."

For the next several days he was intent on a more immediate marriage than we'd hitherto discussed. The prospect both excited and alarmed me: He who rides a tiger cannot dismount.

The third night Malc made dinner for us at Hugh's . . . sausages, mashed potatoes, Graves, Tarragona, and two bottles of a lovely amber Orvieto. After supper we made love cautiously and I agreed on the futility of returning to my hotel.

I had a bath and we finished the third of the four bottles, then, having borrowed one of Betty's gowns, I crawled into bed beside Malc. We argued for a time, because between our nonstop schedule and the combination of wines, I was devoted to the idea of immediate slumber, while Malc was devoted to the idea of immediate amour. We compromised on a respite until 7 A.M. by which time I was at least amenable. He was warm, soft, smooth-skinned, and cuddly as well as terribly unsure, so there was a lot of fumbling and clutching and nuzzling and exploration. No entry, and for me, no resolution.

Malc went out early for firewood and food for breakfast while I cleaned up the room and washed the dishes. It turned into a totally uneventful and really delightful day; seldom had we been so contented or so happy. Betty May returned, radiant, just as we were setting off for the Palladium and an indifferent show.

Later that week, after seeing *Dinner at Eight* and downing several cocktails, Malcolm became drunk and didactic and, of course, we quarreled and separated. He followed me—we made up, and returned to the pub where we ran into another of his "closest friends"—this time the poet, as Malc described him—John Davenport. I recorded my impressions of him later in my diary. "We ended up back at the Cafe Royal where Davenport, who is very flamboyant, very fat, and very anti-Semitic, got into a brawl with a man at the next table who'd objected to some of his remarks. It was a horrid ending to the day and soured me. I've noticed an undercurrent of anti-Semitism among many of Malc's cronies, though he himself is free of it, thank God."

A few days later, Malc having been called out of town, I met with a friend from Berlin's Hegel Haus. We talked of the good old days while visiting the Leicester Galleries, which had an impressive exhibition of Henry Moore, then went on to see some of Epstein's work; our final stop was Hyde Park to hear the orators. For old times sake, we ate schnitzel at a brasserie, and I told him about my love affair with Malc and that we planned to marry. He looked at me, puzzled. "But why an Englishman?" he asked, as though I'd announced my betrothal to a Hottentot.

Next day Malc phoned that he was dining with the poet Edwin Muir, so I attended a concert at the Trinity College of Music and met him afterward. We'd decided to marry in Paris after all, and honeymoon in France and Spain. But with Malcolm at that time nothing was ever peaceful for long, as my diary for the day after records: "The feathers hit the fan again with one of our nastiest quarrels ever. It ended with Malc shouting that he was going to bed with another woman and with me dashing for my bus. I was so hurt and furious I was of a 'that's that!' mind when, on the bus, I felt an arm go round my shoulders and there was Malc. The quarrel was due to my refusal to visit the flat again during the latest absence of Hugh and Betty May." But as usual, once again the storm passed.

"It's all decided," I noted some days later. "I'm leaving for Paris in a week and Malc will join me there by December 31 and we can marry on New Year's, though I can't help wondering whether we shouldn't live together first, like Betty and Hugh, just to be sure we're making no mistake."

That night we went with Betty and Edgell Rickword to Kleinfeld's and the Marquis of Granby and the Plough, and then, Betty insisting, to Smokey Joe's, a non-alcoholic speakeasy-cum-lesbian-pub. Malc brought a bottle and so was broke again, and I grew tired and bored. Next morning he left a note at the Florina: "My darlingest Jan! . . . I write this about half an hour after leaving you, eating a steak pie with your half crown in a thieves' kitchen. It is only to say that I love you and that I shall never love anybody else. Outside, the fiends of Tottenham Court Road are howling in the blackness, imprisoned in the crewless winds. There is comfort in just speaking your name. Oh God, for Paris, with the snow on the ground and ourselves so happy in being, being . . . Jan, don't let's leave each other even in sleep, let us inhabit each other like a cave and creep to each other for the blood that is our strength . . ."

We passed our final night in London at John Davenport's. Blankets were sparse and it was so cold Malc and I slept in our clothes—when we *could* sleep, for John, wrapped nakedly in a blanket on a camp bed, suffered a series of blood-curdling nightmares. At the moment of separation I was seized with sudden panic. At our parting? Our approaching marriage? I knew only that I was about to enter a mysterious world for which I was quite unprepared.

As a parting gift, Malc handed me a small unwrapped piece of Rockingham china, its numerous protuberances meant possibly for rings. There was no room to cram it anywhere so I carried it in my hand, but before I reached France two of its knobby arms had disintegrated, and Immigration sealed its fate by dropping it.

At this juncture, Malcolm had twin obsessions: achieving literary fame and marrying me. I, too, had my obsessions, foremost among them, Malcolm. But headstrong as I was, and romantic and naive, I had a lot to learn.

If I'd imagined arranging a French marriage would entail not more than a few simple documents and locating a romantic inexpensive flat, Paris injected a sharp note of reality. By the third day, our chances of achieving either seemed drowning in formalities: a thirty-day residency; certificates of domicile from each of my stopovers during the past six months; our birth certificates translated, notarized, and presented to innumerable officials; accompanying affidavits for all of the above; on went the list and on. Just getting us to the altar was becoming a life's work!

Clutching a list of available apartments from the American Students and Artists Club, I tramped from Bank to Bank, peering at prohibitively priced Louis Quinze studios, whose johns were in the courtyard, till, on one list, I discovered rue de Cotentin, 32bis. This had belonged to Ben Waring, an early Paris date, and recalling the view and its stark black-and-white chic, I approached it hopefully.

The view, at least, remained. A German couple, now tenanting, wished to sublease for three months starting January 1—500 francs per month for one large room plus bath and kitchenette. The location was convenient. While their furniture was grungy, it would do, and they'd leave us a kitten and possibly a typewriter. Elated, I wrote to Malc, my first ever request for funds: I would need seven pounds.

The next day rained all over my parade: the lawyer's fee abruptly more than doubled, and as for the German couple, they'd scrubbed the charm and were tackling down and dirty. Not only did they demand a ridiculous deposit on their furnishings, but they informed me that my references were "inadequate." Highly insulted, though prudent enough to keep my foot in the door, I told them I would have to let them know.

It helped a little to receive a letter-card from Malc: "God, to hear your laughter again . . ."

And then Julian Trevelyan telephoned. Extravagantly tall and very slender, with an Afro of dark fuzzed hair resembling that of the Guerlain Golliwog, he was a friend of Davenport. To me he became a friend as well during the coming weeks and may likewise have brought me luck, for I now stumbled upon a truly delightful flat. 7, rue Antoine-Chantin offered us a pretty fireplace, a skylight, a lift, a bath, and two rooms with handsome furnishings. At 42 dollars per month, the rent was scarcely more than that of the Waring flat, and there was no comparison. The present occupants, described as an "Anglaise" and her daughter, were expected to leave by Christmas, plenty of time before our wedding date (whenever officialdom decided that might be).

The "Anglaise" was Kathleen Coyle, the Irish writer, tiny, fragile, slender as grass, with huge gray eyes and a voice that drifted away like smoke. When she moved to admit me, I noticed she was lame. "I know we are imposing," she told me in that gentle voice which forced you to strain toward it, "but if we could just remain here through Christmas it would mean so much . . . to be in our own place these last few days . . . We are going to friends, you see . . ."

Her otherworldliness rendered me bumbling and protective. I all but wagged a tail. "It'll be quite all right," I assured her eagerly. "Of course I understand. Through Christmas by all means."

She offered me a tiny glass of cordial, and we sat before the unlit empty fireplace while she spoke of her contractual difficulties: after the publication of *Liv*, she'd signed a contract for eight more books at miserable rates. Now, working day and night to liberate herself, she'd whipped out her latest in just eight days. As I was leaving, she pressed the proofs upon me. "You must let your young Englishman read it. And when I learn where we will be, you must bring him to me."

I read the proofs that evening. They were not very good, I thought, but then what can you do in eight days? Unless, of course, you are God. Or Noel Coward. In years to come I found her name often among the contributors to *Redbook,* so I can only suppose that she won through at last, for gentleness can be as resilient as steel.

That night I celebrated our apartment-to-be with Julian, his girlfriend Louise Scherpenberg, and David Reeves, one of their young friends. After dinner we stopped by the Dôme for drinks and wound up on the rue de Lappe: one thing about Apaches—those real or ersatz Parisian gangster-types—who frequented the cafes there, they certainly could dance.

Malc's first letter was actually a scrawled note in the margins of a tear sheet from the Summer 1933 issue of *Now and Then.* It contained a brief but favorable review of *Ultramarine,* as well as an ad for the book placed by its publishers, Jonathan Cape. (Enclosed too was a money order for three pounds.)

Thrilled at my news about the Waring flat, he directed me now to obtain a receipted bill from the German couple for 1,440 francs per month, instead of the 500 we'd be paying them. His father would then send that amount for rent and we would skim off the difference. Failing their cooperation, I should name myself as landlord.

I couldn't imagine what he was talking about. In money matters I was my mother's daughter—square—but I could just see myself requesting the Germans (who had thought my references "unsatisfactory") arrange a rent receipt for three times what we would pay them. In any case, I was no longer dealing with them and I so wrote Malc. When I returned Kathleen Coyle's proofs I gave her *Ultramarine,* which she promised to show to a French publisher. Perhaps it would make up for the kitten, the Germans, and the 1,440 francs.

In another letter Malc wrote that matters had been "bolloxed up" because Hugh's bank account was overdrawn, which meant that he—Malc—needed to find another "landlord" quickly, though to locate one "sufficiently venal" would be difficult. And then a line, scratched out but decipherable, which in effect read we had better find ourselves new friends. An "odd twist": not only had the Astoria become a nunnery, his passport had been interned within. In closing, he referred again to the defunct MG, hoping that matters could be arranged in time to bring it along to Paris. (There were other references to this phantom car throughout 1934, after which its ghost dematerialized.)

When Mme. Guerzoni, owner of our flat-to-be, drew up my certificate of domicile, she advised me to consider a marriage contract, "to protect yourself in the event of later difficulties." I did not reveal to her that though Tom Forman had described Malc's father as "one of the wealthiest men in England," Malcolm himself hadn't a sou and my endowments were even scantier. The whole idea became quite ludicrous.

Through Julian's support and ingenuity, we finally managed to get my dossier accepted and the wedding set for January 6. It had taken a full month. When Laurence Sterne wrote "They order these things better in France," he certainly was not talking about wedlock.

During that Christmas week, Kathleen Coyle informed me she'd be unable to vacate before the thirty-first. And in a troublesome letter, still in pursuit of this mythical rent receipt, Malcolm enclosed the warning that should my lawyer appear to be a blackmailer or worse, I should cross out his father's address and replace it as I thought best. He then complained, somewhat querulously, about my use of the American Express for mail. Of course, if it was because I was "living at Dicky's" and had not wanted him to know . . . but why? He supposed it was my affair but all the same he hoped I hadn't been because he loved and trusted me absolutely.

"Loved and trusted me absolutely?" I couldn't believe what I was reading. Was this to form the pattern of our married life? This strange idea of trust? In the spring of 1932, Dicky Delano had squired me about

Paris, but I'd seen him only once since my return: he'd talked of his new lady and I'd talked of Malc. "If you're living at Dicky's" indeed! I could have clobbered him.

When I calmed down, I bought Malc's wedding present, a gramophone and a mix of his favorite Joe Venuti and Red Nichols records. Before heading for Julian's Christmas party, I left them at the Hotel Pas de Calais where I'd reserved his room.

Julian's parties were famous and this was in full swing when I discovered that my purse was missing. Our wedding papers were safely at the *mairie* [town hall] and I'd locked my extra cash in my suitcase, but my passport was gone, and because I had neglected to register it at the consulate, its replacement must now come from Washington.

With our wedding less than ten days off was Fate shaking a bony finger? "You've not been listening to me!"

When Malc arrived at the Gare du Nord on December 30, 1933, he was carrying twin ukuleles, one of them for me. Snow fell softly as we left the station. At the Place du Théâtre Français, the fountains played as snowflakes drifted into them. Beyond stretched the holiday fairyland of the Avenue de l'Opéra.

We consummated our reunion at the Hotel Pas de Calais, joyously rediscovering one another, talking nonstop, and making love. Later we played the gramophone, and spun delicious fantasies.

"Malc arrived . . . looking marvelous in complete new clothes," I later wrote. "It was so perfect seeing him again that I burst into tears. It had snowed and is snowing still . . . a harbinger of good."

Some hours later we strolled to the *mairie* on which our *banns* were posted. Clarence Malcolm Lowry, of Inglewood, Caldy, Cheshire, England, born July 28, 1909, and Janine van der Heim of Bayside, Long Island, New York, born June 11, 1911. (That was the true spelling of my father's name: often on tour, he later simplified it.) I had to dissuade Malcolm from removing the yellow *affiche* and bearing it reverently away.

We were to meet Julian and his party at the Dôme for New Year's Eve. Spotting him, I waved frantically at the pirate in a bright sash, a turban, and one of Louise's earrings.

"My God," Malc muttered. "He does look Montparnasse! Who are the bearded ladies with him?"

"The blond one's Brock, a painter friend of Julian's, but I don't know the others." Brock wore a silk neckerchief instead of a shirt. Beneath his wide Svengali hat his lips looked blue.

"Well see who's here at last! Welcome to Paris, Malc!" And snagging a waiter as he greeted me, Julian secured a table and ordered a round of Pernods. His entourage scraped into seats, banter and laughter coursing like electricity. When the Pernods arrived, Malc knocked his back without adding water and looked vaguely surprised as it hit his throat.

"That stuff's not bitters," Julian cautioned mildly. "It'll get there in a rush."

"I'll have another then," and Malc signaled the *garçon.* Julian caught my eye and shrugged but the arrival of Louise created a diversion. Nearly as tall as Julian, a husky-voiced New Yorker whose tilted eyes suggested rather the outreaches of Mongolia, she was irreverent, direct, and easy in her skin. I'd liked her from the start.

"You must be Malcolm . . . I'm Louise," she hailed him. "Well, Malcolm, aren't you going to say hello?"

"Have a drink," Malcolm said instead but, in response to mingled greetings, Louise began to circulate. Malc finished his second drink and turned to me with determination. "Janl," he said, "let's go."

"Go where? We just got here. I'm still on my first drink."

He took my glass and drained it. "We'll have one somewhere else. Let's go."

I put out my hand to check him. "It's New Year's Eve and we're invited to Julian's party. Please, Malcolm, don't spoil everything."

"But I want to be alone with you," he insisted, "the two of us, *just* the two of us. This is a bloody farce."

Could he hate Paris merely because I loved it? "We've all our lives to be alone together, but this is New Year's Eve. And everyone else is having fun." He shrugged my hand away and when we all moved on to La Corbeille, amid the toasts to our impending marriage, we picked solemnly at our food and morosely swallowed the harsh and sour wine. Afterwards, our group segmented, most of them party-bound, and we found ourselves back at the Dôme, resentful and alone at a small table.

"You can have all the bloody-minded celebrations you've a mind to but you can count me *out!* I'm *not* going on to Julian's."

"Oh Malcolm, you've spoiled just everything!" I jumped to my feet. "I don't understand you! I don't understand what's happening to us." And before he should see that I was crying, I turned and ran downstairs. In the euphoria of our pending marriage, I discounted our many arguments and quarrels in Wales and London, assuring myself all that had been *before.*

When I returned, Malcolm had disappeared. I sat before the pile of saucers wondering how this could be the New Year's Eve I'd dreamed about and what to do. Then Julian returned, attended by the inevitable Brock. "Where the hell has Malcolm got to? We're all ready to leave."

"Malc isn't going. I don't know where he is."

"Downstairs, probably," Julian said. "Anyhow, you come along with us. I'll see if I can find him." He went off and Brock asked, "Sweet Lord Jesus, is Malcolm always like this? What in God's name are you marrying him for?"

"Oh shut up." I said miserably. "I'm sorry, Brock. I don't know what's got into him."

"I guess he'll be okay," Brock said without conviction.

When Julian rejoined us, he was looking harassed. "Malcolm's downstairs all right but he won't come up. I can't do a thing with him. What's got into him, Jan?"

"You've known him longer than I; you were at Cambridge with him." And at Cambridge, I knew, Malc had been something of a legend. At this point Louise located us.

"I've got to dash home and get into my gypsy rags. You coming? Everybody will be there except us." When she heard about Malcolm, she said, "I'll get him up. I bet you I'll get him up."

"But he's in the men's room." Julian protested.

Louise laughed, her eyes glittering. "Why Julian! And before everybody, too!" Then she strode toward the stairs calling back, "Anyhow, watch my technique!"

She returned with Malcolm five minutes later. They were laughing and she had her arm about his waist. "Malcolm's all right," she said. "He's coming with us to the party. Here, Julian, take him around and let him pick out what he wants to drink." She waited for me and said, "Poor Malcolm's all washed up. He shouldn't have had so many Pernods."

"He'll have more before the evening's through," I said glumly. "What did you say to him?"

"Told him I'd spank his bottom for him. He's just a little boy and he wants to be kidded along. I think he's terribly ashamed of himself."

We didn't say any more on the subject. When we reached the studio, a mob was already celebrating. Someone was playing the piano; streamers and serpentine paper hung from the gallery railing and from the ceiling; it was Brock, I learned, who had covered the walls with felt abstractions depicting the surrender of Persephone (a pink felt curve) to Pluto (a metal bar). Multicolored balloons, ready for release, had been crammed into a closet off the gallery; easels had disappeared; in one corner they'd arranged a couch to tempt *les amoureaux*. On the far wall, three tribal African instruments surrounded the anomaly of a ukulele.

"It'll be a good party if the accordionist ever gets here," Louise said. "Otherwise Julian will be frantic." Brock joined us and we drank red wine while Louise changed to her gypsy rags. Then Malc arrived with Julian and, spotting the ukulele, attacked a bawdy favorite song of his, "The Bastard King of England," with much gusto.

When the accordionist appeared, he was not the man Julian had hired, but an agile little Italian who explained why he was replacing his "sick friend." Julian eyed him apprehensively and tried to describe his plans for the balloons. "At midnight, Luigi, you must take them from the closet up there where you'll be playing. Cut them apart and toss them over the railing. D'you have a watch?"

"Oui, monsieur," said Luigi, looking sleepy and owlish but with an obvious effort at attention.

"Damn him!" Julian watched the little musician weave toward his post on the gallery. "He's pissed as all get out. I hope he lasts the night."

Luigi began playing up a storm and Louise took Julian's arm. "He's good, though," she commented happily.

I danced with an ersatz Apache whose hands were everywhere till Malc bawled "How do you like my femme?" Unlike a true Apache, mine became frightened and abandoned his swoops and dives and me.

During one of Luigi's breaks, Malc and the ukulele performed anew, this time "Gethusalem" and "St. Louis Blues." The party seemed to be going well. But later I attempted a Russian dance I'd learned when I was eight . . . the one where you sit on your heels, arms folded, and kick out alternately. A man in a chef's hat joined me and there was some stamping and clapping in accompaniment, till Malcolm poured his glass of wine over us both, announcing "I now pronounce you man and wife." No one laughed much at that and I stuttered, "Oh Malc, you fool! My dress!" But as I stood up, I grabbed his arm: a wave of nausea had gripped me.

"Malcolm, I think I'm sick." He hurried me out into the sharp December night where the cold air began to clear my head. "Let's go home now," I urged when I could speak. "It's been a horrid night."

"But it isn't midnight yet. It isn't New Year's yet. You wanted New Year's Eve, remember? Besides, I need a drink and you should certainly lie down." He dragged me back inside, settled me on the couch intended *pour les amoureaux,* and for a time I dozed. When I sat up, he seemed to have disappeared; beside me sat Brock's cousin.

"You feeling okay now?" I wasn't but I nodded shakily. Brock's cousin placed an arm about my shoulders as support. "Would you like water or a drink or anything?"

Before I could reply, Malcolm loomed over us. "I play the ukulele to entertain my wife's friends while she fornicates in a corner!" he announced angrily.

"Fornicates?" I echoed, *"This?"*

Brock's cousin snatched his arm away. "You know what, Malc, you're crazy!" His voice rose suddenly as Malcolm yanked him to his feet. "Let go of me, you crazy bastard," he yelled, but Malcolm slung him across the room where he skidded into the stove and grabbed at the stovepipe. It broke loose, pouring a shower of soot into the studio. There was a moment of shocked silence, then a woman screamed. Brock ran to his cousin's aid.

Julian seized Malc and shouted, "You damned fool, you might have killed him!" Both Brock and his cousin had scorched their hands on the stovepipe.

Then came a strangled wail from the accordion and Louise cried, "Oh my God! Watch out!" For Luigi, struggling both with his gala of balloons and to interpret the confrontation going on below now over-reached the railing. For an unavailing moment he wobbled desperately, then plummeted like some huge astounded baby still clinging to its Brobdingnagian toys. The accordion unloosed a long descending fart.

In the ensuing babble, Malc headed for the door. I pulled myself together and ran after him. From varying quarters came the blare of horns heralding 1934. Malcolm, when I caught up with him, was smiling tightly, ever responsive to grotesquerie. His glance was challenging. "So much for the New Year's Eve!" he said. "And New Year's celebrations." For a long moment we stared at one another, the cacophonous horns an obbligato to our wariness.

〜 〜 〜

Kathleen Coyle may have been frail but she was a survivor. We were unable to gain access to our apartment till January 3. When we rolled up, it was to find David Reeves with the cigarettes and stockings I'd asked him to bring from London. He helped us carry up our bags, after which we went to Prater's for hors d'oeuvres.

January 6, Epiphany, dawned grayly. Malc, who could not sleep under a skylight, had opted for the small bedroom, and as the alarm pealed he emerged from his lair, yawning and yanking at his pajama cord. I was bedded down on the living room couch, and he sat on its edge looking rumpled and slightly flushed.

"Well it's here. Happy wedding day." We smiled nervously at one another. "Jan, you *are* sweet. Don't get up yet. We've loads of time."

"Don't forget we have to pick up Julian and Louise. Besides, there's my missing passport. We'd better be a little early just in case."

"I wish to God I spoke French." He rubbed his head between his hands. "Will I have to answer a beastly lot of questions?"

"Just signing papers I think, though probably a lot."

"It sounds so bloody dreary." He nuzzled my neck. "Your hair's all curly, Jan! How *nice* you are to wake to." As he slipped one arm about me, the concierge's knock, late as we had known it would be, summoned us.

"Merci, Madam," I called. *"Ça va."*

"Gelatinous old Fate" Malcolm complained. He looked suddenly very young and vulnerable. "I promise that I'll make you happy, Mrs. Lowry. I really can, you know." So far we'd kept our promise not to mention New Year's Eve.

While he was in the bath, I made the beds and laid out my wedding clothes. I'd found the hand-knit dress in Vienna the previous year and was still proud of it. We were nearly ready when Malcolm discovered that both gray ties he'd brought along had disappeared. We rummaged madly, losing patience, snapping at one another until, frustration giving way to laughter, Malcolm held out his arms. "Hold me," I begged. "I'm simply scared to death."

"I know. We both are. But it'll all work out, you'll see. Remember, Jan, we were meant for one another."

Nervously holding hands for reassurance, we set off to collect our witnesses and after a round of brandies to steady everybody, arrived at the gaunt and ugly *mairie* of the 14th Arrondissement. (It is now, by the way, quite a lovely building.) Directed to a small drab room containing fading portraits of some former mayors, we found a motley collection of the affianced already there. No one looked happy; the atmosphere fostered apprehension, even for a lame official in a dusty uniform who lurked by the door. "To make sure nobody escapes," Louise whispered irreverently. In her fringed plaid skirt she resembled photographs of the sultry Lenore Ulric playing Kiki.

Half a dozen documents were presented for our signatures. Repeatedly I wrote my maiden then my married name. Once I wrote Jan instead of Janine which promptly elicited censure. "Partout la meme chose, mademoiselle. Signez partout la meme!"

The *Salle de Mariage* across the hall was large, ornate, and imitation gothic. Its carved pews had been stained walnut and at the front four thronelike chairs faced a dais and the mayoral bench. Our names being the first called, we were directed to the "thrones." Behind us waited fourteen couples and their witnesses, many in wedding garb, in prelude to religious ceremonies yet to come. The sad little dresses looked skimpy and ill-fitting, with veils which could have been mosquito netting. One bride-to-be was crying, her face—swollen by tears—had acquired the puffed-up appearance of a turnip. Beside her, her groom looked angry and indomitable—trapped.

"How awful," Louise whispered. "Like something out of Zola." The groom's angry scowl forced her attention elsewhere. "Look at the murals," she whispered then, indicating panels in the style of Puvis de Chavannes, each one a hymn to domesticity and motherhood.

After a string of manifestoes had been read, the mayor first summoned our witnesses in error; the situation clarified, we all four stood before him for the ceremony. At the obligatory question "Do you take this woman?" Malcolm, who had not understood one word, looked absolutely stunned. The mayor repeated it, testily, whereupon Louise and Julian, prompting in unison, loudly whispered "*Oui.*" As one all but comatose, Malcolm echoed it, the word emerging in a loud and startled snort.

It was now my turn, and I caught with dismay the inclusion of "obey;" I had been hoping for contemporary vows. When all four of us had fulfilled our roles, amid a final spate of French, an official ran to us with a tin plate and said loudly, "Pour les pauvres."

"At last a familiar phrase," Malcolm remarked.

Our marriage certificate was a booklet which contained fourteen pages for recording births.

Julian and Louise gave us a wedding lunch, after which, since we ourselves were having a tentative soiree the following evening, I shopped at Uniprix for necessities—our joint possessions numbering only books and clothes. Over and over I repeated my new names; Mrs. Malcolm Lowry, Jan Lowry, Jan Gabrial Lowry . . . how beautiful they sounded. The morning had transformed me into *wife*, and the isolation in which I'd previously lived would be absorbed into warmth and unity of that small word *we*.

So I shopped happily, wrapped in the cotton wool of expectation.

In the days ahead I made many discoveries which roused my curiosity. For one, Malc wore a silver-colored medallion. In recent years medals and chains have enjoyed a vogue, but in 1934 they were mainly limited to the Catholic countries, and Malcolm was neither Catholic nor churchly.

I tried to sound offhand. "What's that?"

He explained it was a gift from Margo, wife of his favorite brother, a lady prone to sessions with a Ouija board. The medallion was an Italian coin which had been the talisman of her seagoing grandfather to whom Malc referred as The Old Man, or, variously, O.C. (Old Captain). "The Old Man loves us both," he explained, soberly. "He will be our adviser."

"You don't mean he's still alive?"

"Good Lord, no. He died years ago. But Margo can get in touch with him at any time."

Alarmed at the prospect of a future charted by the family ghost, I voiced a protest. "But I don't know your Margo. I've never seen a Ouija board but I don't believe in them." A tactless comment which produced a spat.

But the Ouija board was only the tip of an impressive iceberg, for Malc was totally fascinated by the inexplicable: tarot cards (the Hanged Man, hanged upside down because he saw the truth); Charles Fort's tales of frogs raining on London, toads on France, or red worms upon Halmstad; and above all by Peter Ouspensky whose *Tertium Organum* and *New Model of the Universe* were ever close at hand. Being of a fairly rational disposition, I could not help wondering what sort of oddly obsessed man I had just married.

Through Kathleen Coyle, the *Nouvelle Revue Française* became interested in *Ultramarine,* even suggesting likely translators. Ours was by no means the Paris of the twenties for it was a period of gathering tensions, but as Malc had written me of London, "There is certainly life there when tavern doors are on the swing." From England we received a glowing review of *Ultramarine* by Hamish Miles, lauding it as one of the most striking works of fiction that had come his way. It was a forerunner of the accolades that were to greet *Volcano.*

Our first weeks demanded varying adjustments. In Malcolm I found a man who, small though his sex might be, was desperately eager to satisfy me and he did. Since none of my fleeting loves had seemed mindful of the purpose of a clitoris, doubtless dismissing it as one of nature's leftovers, in those initial weeks we were discovering together the sweet intimacy which can follow orgasm, no matter how induced.

Still and all, this did not prevent Malcolm from attacking me during our violent quarrels. One subject and one subject only would remain out of bounds: his writing and my own. On all else, it was open season. After one such set-to, when we'd stormed separately from the apartment, I returned to find an angry scrawl berating me for "psycho-sexual impotence."

Malc did not come home that night. I walked around until 4 A.M. The flat felt empty and unnaturally still and I grew panicky. Before leaving, Malcolm had grabbed a wad of paper, shouting that he would finish off his letters "like the Japanese" before they died. Every odd action of his returned to haunt me. I was certain he'd killed himself. For two hours I lay terrified, sure he was dead. Had I ever comprehended how frantically I loved him? Horrible visions mocked me. I visited the morgue. I appealed to the Prefecture. If only he'd return, I vowed I would be voiceless. Then came the creaking of the lift. The house was so still it sounded like a groan. I felt I could live until it reached our floor. There followed an endless wait, then a key fumbled at the lock and I lay very still. I was afraid for myself now, afraid that Malcolm, when he was that drunk, might harm me.

At last he entered and hovered a few moments at my bedside. I didn't dare to breathe. For a long moment he fumbled at the covers. Then he said "Dormez. Le diable est mort," and veered away from me into the other room. And I hated him suddenly. I hated him so terribly that I wished he had died so that I might have gone on loving him.

And then at eight o'clock he had gone out again.

That evening I was getting into my black dress when the doorbell rang. I was so certain that it would be Malc, that he had lost his key, that when I opened the door my face was totally expressionless. But it wasn't Malc.

It was David Reeves, holding his little suitcase. He looked very young and vulnerable and very tired. The hard lump which had formed in my throat on hearing the bell dissolved. David entered and asked if Malc were there. "I've got to find him. When I left him earlier, he said he'd come straight here."

"Why is it so important?"

"It's Julian and Louise . . . they've separated and Julian's all shot up. He's talking about suicide and I hoped Malc might be able to talk to him."

I closed the door and stared at him. "You can't be serious! Not Julian and Louise?"

He eased down on the couch. "That isn't all," he said. "Louise is in love with Brock, and they are going to Spain together."

"But Brock is their best friend. It's totally insane! How can she fall in love with . . . David! He's just a baby!"

"Not such a baby," David said. "And she's been in love some time only she didn't know it. Neither did Brock. Julian was the only one who saw it coming. He said, "You've got a kick in the pants for me tonight, haven't you?"

He towed the little suitcase, which fell over. "I've been trying to give her my school sweater. She wanted a white one and I said I'd give her mine."

It was raining hard and the wind blew gusts sharply against the windowpanes and thudded on the skylight. Then, like an obbligato, the creaking of the mounting *ascenseur* penetrated the room. I should tell David to go out and down the stairs, I thought, except that it would have sounded melodramatic. The clanging of the iron grille was followed presently by the fumbling key around the unlocked door.

When he saw David, Malcolm stopped. His eyebrows jerked. Then he came in and shut the door, leaning back against it. He was very wet and there was a dusting of sugar down his coat and at his trouser cuffs.

"Bonswar." He bowed elaborately and pulled a paper sack from his pocket. "Sugar." Through a hole in the bag, sugar sifted onto the floor and into small puddles of rain water which were forming. "And *aourt*." He shrugged off his coat, dropping it on the table, ignoring it when it slid off.

With exaggerated heartiness, he gripped David's shoulder and shook it, amused and contemptuous. "How you?"

"Malc, I came here to look for you. Julian's all smashed to pieces. Louise is going to Spain with Brock. Can't you think of anything we can do to help?"

Malcolm's attention was wandering. He was staring now at me. "Who?"

"Julian."

"Why?"

"Louise has left him," I said. "She's going to Spain with Brock. Julian's all broken up."

"Julian's all right," Malcolm said. His hand moved over David's head, almost caressingly. "So? Was it a nice evening?"

"I've only been here ten minutes. I wanted to find you. I thought I should tell you about Louise and Julian . . ."

"S'matter with'm?"

David sighed. He didn't answer. When Malcolm loosed his grip and wandered over to the table which held the gramophone, David stood up, grasping his little suitcase. Winding the gramophone, Malc didn't look around as David left the room.

A few days later we had another bruising onslaught after which I downed Pernods defiantly and passed out. Being Malc, he left another note. This one informed me that he had raped me and I had eagerly responded, proving thus, in my sleep, that I did really love him and also that "no woman is raped against her will." He'd wait for me to join him at the Dôme, so we could "do something exciting." Meantime he'd left the fire on and the sheets turned down.

Had the episode ever actually occurred? I had no memory of it. Could it be that this was Malcolm's means of saving face by reasserting that it was only our love for one another which ultimately mattered?

On the evening of January 29 he met with a prospective translator, so I went off alone to a Lilian Harvey film. It may have been the sentimental tale, or missing him beside me in the theatre, but walking home, emotion flooded me. To share my life with that extraordinary intellect must surely overbalance our periodic outbursts; so, too, must Malcolm's wit and magnetism, and his capacity for tenderness.

Neither of us would forget that night, for it was then we achieved our first triumphant mating. Such unquenchable gaiety overwhelmed us that we clung together, crying and laughing, making up new songs, exulting in our oneness—now at last so total—convinced we had indeed been born for one another even as Malcolm had so often written me. How confident, how very sure we were that lovely night.

In April I was to return to New York to visit mother while Malcolm would take advantage of my absence by going to England to inform his parents of our marriage. As soon as feasible thereafter, he'd arrange for my return and we'd spend our delayed honeymoon in the south of France. Our plan was joyous as sunlight, and as evanescent.

At Fontenay-aux-Roses, a small village near Paris, we initiated our nonsense songs. I'd make them up as we went along, adding verses as they occurred to me, the sillier the better. The child in each of us warmed to their foolishness.

I am a pusscat, you are a pupdog, we are a familee-ee-ee

We will go sailing, probably baling, over a bright blue sea . . .

We too will wander, never asunder, yowling ineffablee-ee-ee..

I am a pusscat, you are a pupdog, we are a familee-ee-ee . . .

"Never lose that adorable side of your nature," Malc would urge. (Besides Pusscat, he endowed me with a variety of nicknames which included Starkey, Trundlebug, and above all Rainbowpuss.)

Toward mid-February we went to Chartres, which I'd not visited since being bodily ejected from the bicycle shop. Our trip had a wobbly start. On the day scheduled, it poured, and the next day dawned no brighter. Toward afternoon, Malcolm insisted we leave anyhow. "Go out in this?" I pointed at the skylight where rain beat an intense tattoo. "Besides, look at the time."

"We can stay overnight. Or several nights. What difference does it make?"

"Getting soaked doesn't seem such a bright idea. I'm just over one awful cold."

"Well wear your boots and raincoat," he said reasonably. "Besides, it's probably not raining there." Then, seeing I still hesitated, "Suit yourself then. I'm going anyhow." His face had clouded over like the day. Huffing into his coat, the door slammed after him. In such senseless ways had our quarrels often had their genesis.

I stood briefly by the window, indecision rendering me jittery, but finally snatched my rain gear and hurried to catch up. Later that spring he wrote "Hotel Room in Chartres," which recognizes both the ambivalence in Malcolm and our too-frequent inflexibility with one another. For Malcolm it was a productive spring; he wrote steadily and achieved half a dozen successful submissions, as well as planned a novel to be set in Paris. More and more we were adjusting to the demands of writing—the need for simplification, the control, always the control over one's chosen subject.

⌐◡ ◡ ◡

Shortly after our return, a poster claimed that James Joyce would attend a meeting of Les Amis de 1914. Sylvia Beach thought the idea improbable and Malc, though Joyce was among his major influences, considered the claim unfounded and preposterous. Curious, however, I decided to go anyway, and trundled off alone, arranging to meet Malc later on at La Rotonde. Oddly enough, Joyce did indeed show up, but that was all he did. The famous Irish voice remained unheard. Behind his glasses could it be that he was not awake? We broke up around eleven, but not before some minor artists from the Odéon had declaimed. Badly. I set off to amuse my husband with a description of the evening and the roof fell in.

Malcolm was twenty minutes late, and when he finally arrived, seemed noticeably preoccupied. Not until we were served did he address me, and then, regarding me dispassionately, he announced: "I think you should go back to America. You were going in April anyway. I think you should leave at once. Or I shall."

He had, he told me coldly, discovered my European diaries and had read them. I stared at him. "That was a dirty thing to do." My breath was barely audible.

He shrugged. "I should have known all about them sometime, I suppose. I only wonder that with your philosophy of 'sincerity' you didn't tell me yourself."

"Those diaries were private. They were personal journals. And they were my own affair. You violated them."

"Your own *affairs,* you mean." We stared at one another angrily. "I'm going back to sea," he then announced, looking past and away from me.

"Bon voyage," I said tonelessly. My hands shook as I fumbled with my coat. When had I married the Grand Inquisitor?

As I plunged toward the Odéon metro, I tried to remember what it was I'd written, recalling in dismay my thoughtless comments on his undeveloped sex, written when in Granada, and some subsequent notes on my own lack of ardor.

But even that was not the worst. In a further notebook, had I not described Werner, met while in Barcelona, dwelt on our unfulfilled desires—unfulfilled because of Malcolm's letters—and added something to the effect that he, Werner, could probably satisfy a woman to the point of unconsciousness? Could Malcolm have gorged himself on that as well? And what about Berlin? I had filled six notebooks in all, romantic, opinionated, callow, unedited, and—God help me—detailed. Had Malcolm found time to read all six of them?

Too shocked for tears or rational decisions, and too cold to wander, I returned to our apartment. At a little after two, Malcolm returned, threw his coat on the couch, and sat across from me. He looked pale, but mercifully, he was sober. "Look here," he began, "how serious is this anyway?"

I shook my head. "Surely that's up to you."

"Oh, Jan, say that it doesn't matter. Not between us. It was the thought of you and other people, doing the things that somehow belonged to us. But we can't let that matter. Look, Jan, say that it doesn't . . ."

"If it matters to you it matters," I said numbly.

"No, not like that. Don't say it like that. I really love you terribly. It makes a fool of me at times, but I'll get over it. Please, Jan, it doesn't really matter what I said?"

"Of course that doesn't matter, but what about my diaries?"

"Forget the damn diaries," Malcolm said. "I shouldn't have read them. It was wrong of me. But I was so damned hurt . . ."

"Oh my God," I said, "I never meant to hurt you. You must know now it isn't true, the thing I wrote about you in Granada . . ."

"It's true enough," Malcolm said. "All my life I've been sniggered at because my damn cock is so small. It's just that I couldn't bear to think that you too . . . Look, Starkey, I *do* make you happy that way, don't I? Only don't say yes if it isn't so."

We held each other tightly once again, much as we had on that fulfilling night such a short while ago, though what we now felt was not exhilaration but a clinging need akin to desperation. Somberly we agreed it was something else we'd forget, something else not to be referred to.

As a fresh start, we set out for Rouen, with its old quaint streets, its ancient marketplace, and the hotel with the purple thistles on the orange paper and the great wide bed. To us Rouen was to become a symbol, the place where we began the healing process and licked each other's wounds.

↝ ↝ ↝

On March 2 I wrote Louise in Malaga, where she and Brock were staying.

> I'm returning our debts to you both with many thanks. David dashed up yesterday to say he'd had an S.O.S. from your direction. Unfortunately it all got pretty complicated. Malc and I were making love on the sofa—very undraped—when the bell rang. I thought it was probably the concierge so we didn't move. Much. Then by some mischance, having apparently left the door unlatched, our Mysterious Visitor pushed it open. We both howled and the M.V. fled. Later the concierge gave us a note, from David, rambling, vague, and shaken, and the only part of it which made sense was the news that you are broke . . . I hope only momentarily.
>
> All else apart, how are you and is it really love? Paris seems deserted, so we lead very quiet lives, are working hard, and see few people.
>
> We've been to Chartres and to Rouen (and oh the thrill of a full-sized bed after these damned cots)! All is once again going smoothly though there was an awfully tense situation some days ago. Malc found my European diaries and our union threatened to come to a crashing unmendable end—Malc to head off to sea once more and I

to go who knew where?—but we couldn't stick it and we reconciled, very emotionally, and the next day went off to Rouen. Perhaps we are finally learning to love and accept each other as we are.

My sailing date was set for April 3—almost exactly two years since I'd left New York. Then on March 20 I became unwell, but only sketchily. The possibility confronting us appeared gargantuan. In a mere two weeks, I should be en route home. Hopeful, confused, and troubled, we discussed alternatives.

"It's those damned condoms," Malcolm said; "the way they keep slipping off. I know we've been choosing names and all that, and there's absolutely nothing I want more than a child of yours—ours—but darling, the timing couldn't possibly be worse! My old man doesn't even know I'm married. He'd cut us off without a farthing. You and I haven't any money, and as for *Ultramarine,* well, forget *Ultramarine.* I can't be the one to tell you what to do, Starkey—it's you who'll have the pain in any case—but we do have our whole lives ahead of us, my rainbowpuss . . . "

He put his arms about me, comforting us both. "You're all the child I really want for now—my child and my wife and my trundlebug. And we'll be a familee-ee-ee yet, I promise you . . ."

This year, next year, some time, never . . .

But he was right, of course. The timing, after all, was rotten. As he'd said.

I entered a clinic on March 27 and Malc wrote three tender letters. He had the same heartsickness as when he first fell in love with me, but now that I was his wife it was multiplied a hundredfold. Would I forgive his boorishness and suspiciousness and remember only Chartres and all our lovely times? . . . he was only a "goddamn writing-paper lover"— that he knew, but while I was in the States he'd get his life straight, work hard, and blaze our trail . . . I was far grander than anyone he knew and he promised me sun and sea for all my life, and that he'd look after me . . . be more than "an affable ghost who had the misfortune to be virile . . . " Soon it would be Easter—"the day that Christ got up" as I'd called it, and we too would resurrect.

On April 3 we departed for Le Havre where I boarded the *Ile de France*. Our trip was shadowed by the imminence of separation, though we expected to reunite in just nine weeks and leave for Villefranche in the South of France. Bolstered by our dreams, we outlined together the story of "In Le Havre."

Mother met me at the New York dock, smaller, older, and whiter than I'd remembered, her face pugnacious and questing. But I could not confide in her now, and yet there were no words for all I owed her.

Europe had given me confidence and poise. To my selfless mother, her child had seen a world she'd never visit, but which she had made possible by her sacrifices. For nearly 23 years she had supported me. ("You didn't ask to come into this world." How often had I heard her turn gratitude aside with just those words!) Though I was able, ultimately, to contribute to her livelihood, here, too, she'd remained self-sufficient and deposited all my checks, unspent, in the careful savings she would leave me. Throughout my life, her love had been my strength; she would not have it otherwise in death.

When I reached New York, I promptly presented copies of several of Malcolm's stories to the Ann Watkins agency and placed two with Whit Burnett's *Story* magazine. (It was Burnett who had recommended the Watkins agency.)

Our intended nine weeks' separation lost all meaning as the date for our reunion wobbled. During the nearly four months we were to be apart, Malcolm wrote me lengthy devoted and tormented letters—very short, however, on specifics. Months later I would learn that for much of this period he was, bluntly, drunk. Neglecting to pay for the utilities or the cleaning woman, he lost those services, and the damage he brought onto Mme. Guerzoni's pretty apartment while in his cups would invoke both the demands of Madame's solicitors and his father's ire.

Finally, contrary to all we'd planned together, our weathercock spun toward a reunion in the States. It proved a fatal turning. Forsaking sun and gentle seaside villages, we tumbled instead into the maelstrom of New York.

Entr'acte

Nothing is so interesting as passion, because everything in it is unexpected.

The ardour of love increases through suspicion and the jealousy which comes from it.

Lack of confidence makes a lover suspect sinister things of his beloved.

Prudery is a kind of avarice, the worst of all.

—Stendhal, "On Love"

From Paris Malcolm sent me "In Le Havre" and "Hotel Room in Chartres." Ann Watkins had now agreed to represent Malcolm in America and had put him into the hands of Harold Matson, who would later take him to his own agency. Though they were unable to place "In Le Havre," Whit Burnett bought "Chartres" for *Story*, which, however, disappointed Malcolm who had hoped for *Vanity Fair*.

During our separation we wrote constantly, impatient with the time it took letters to arrive, there being as yet no planes to span the seas. Many of Malcolm's were written from our rue Antoine-Chantin flat and in the first, covering seven pages, he confessed to feeling like a jungle cat deprived now of its cub. We could have enjoyed Le Havre together . . . its waterfront cafes with the same salt-sea ambience as those in the West Indies . . .

Mingled with tenderness for our memories were regrets for the times he'd been intolerant, yet such upheavals had only strengthened love; he'd banish his goblins of self-pity and self-indulgence yet, become the husband and the comrade I had sought. At home as I now was with a mother who cherished me, I must not forget my other home in Europe, deep in a man's heart. "Ah, Ruelle de la Demi-Lune, where love was everything and memory, like a muted string, is hushed and small . . ."

His attitude toward contraceptives had been ill conceived, he now admitted; never would we confront *that* problem, but oh the torment till he'd fully satisfied me and then—oh God—how gentle a mistress and how enchanting a wife! Our love was bound to surmount death itself for even in the grave we two would find a way to "there embrace."

"John henry" was sick with *sehnsucht* and aching day and night. He promised to be the best lover I had ever had, longing above all else to be the most fulfilling of lovers to me. Adjustments, always difficult at first, seldom resolved so beautifully as had ours. No son or friend could ever mean so much for I was daughter and mistress, his comrade and his friend.

He wrote that he'd be signing a second contract with the *Nouvelle Revue Française* for a projected book to be called *So We Live Forever Taking Leave.* Its stories would create a novel of farewell, ending with "Hotel Room in Chartres." "Meantime, a beach in Spain or France or Italy arches its back with desire for us . . ."

He'd been rereading all my letters there in our Paris, where life came into being with a birth-agony forgotten in the ecstasy of its fulfillment. Our love, my loveliness, still haunted that small room. Did I remember our first orgasm together when we'd sung "Blue Skies," and I'd made up a song called "Running Away From Myself" and he'd promised not to do so but he did anyway and so did I? . . . But it was always love, in spite of my apprehensions and my sufferings, in spite of his mistrust and accusations, it was always love in that lifetime we had shared in that small room which I still filled . . .

"Be my whore, my mistress! I'll be unfaithful to you with yourself . . ." But it was wonderful to know I was his wife, though what he felt also was that "passionate friendship which man is said to feel for man" which I described as "comradeship," though never had he felt it for anyone till now." All my friends live with strangers and lose their souls." It had been wonderful to find me inside "so soft and yielding." I was a *niña* but I was a woman too. He'd been little more than an adolescent, fumbling and maladroit, but now he had matured: he had achieved his manhood. Would I "do my rabbit" for him?

Exulting in the news of the second *N.R.F.* contract, I tried to let him know how proud I was: "My darling husband, we'll be together very soon. We must! In Spain or Italy or the sun-brightness of the Côte d'Azur, but anywhere, anywhere, I promise to be whatever will enthrall you, be it your joyous mistress, be it your willing whore—for we are all-in-all to one another. Lawrence says a man becomes polygamous when a part has been given but not the whole, and a woman when a part has been taken but not the whole. Only *believe* in me . . . know that I am ever and always totally your Jan . . ."

And from Malc: "Starkey, a year ago in Granada . . . life suddenly seems a short while in which to get to know someone as lovely as you . . . Remember the man who was clever enough to trap for a moment the Southwest wind in her swift lovely voyage through the stars and heavens. A year ago in Granada . . ."

Yet his next letters lashed out, bitter and unhappy, from a hotel near Chartres and probably from Malcolm in his cups . . . feeling abandoned, his socks undarned, the bills unpaid, "electric light people dancing in a row, cheating . . ." Madame apparently fed up; the cleaning woman a truant; "water temperature beastly, cobwebs *partout;* heat cut off; heart cut off; clock pas vrai; gramophone broken—Paris bloody, bloody, bloody" without me, so that he literally never wanted to see it again . . . never!

He wondered whether I might not be more content with someone to whom all the attributes came more readily, someone with money and influence and lands and the butler to hand me my pen or tray; someone respected above all instead of "this Dostoevskian creature, the clown in *King Lear,* the strong man in the zoo . . ." "I waked this morning in a large clean bed, looking onto green slim trees like you, and I saw how it would be turning over to each other naked and young, with sunlight . . . and flowing into each other endlessly."

I'd written of an idea I'd had to hitch-hike through the Balkans; he seized upon it eagerly: ". . . I can't write, I've quite forgotten how to write, I'm quite content to be the husband of Jan Gabrial . . . my ambition is now limited to learning how to pitch a tent on the frontiers of Bulgaria . . . All tenderness, all spring and summer to you, the only girl in the world . . ."

He longed to penetrate my bones . . . to see me as for the first time, and to ravish me. We would meet again and I would be submissive for his body would melt the iceberg I'd once written that he made of mine—would melt it into "boiling lava." Without anger he longed to do me an "exquisite violence," to feel my breasts respond, to ravish and then to comfort me . . .

Could he not be to me the "week-end lover? the delicious adventurer? the escape as well as the reality, sufficing for a single time, a solitary place? My God, you once actually had to say to me, 'Say to yourself, *I desire this woman.*' My Christ!"

Following a period when I heard absolutely nothing, a note of aggravation crept into my July 7 letter. "I love and miss you like all hell but please for God's sake stop sending cables that don't say anything and send a letter, even if all it contains is an address, so I can at least think of you as being SOMEWHERE!... Let's please go back to Rouen to the waterfront cafe where we found the dancing bear and where we looked at a black river afterward and wandered among bridges and missed the train and spent the night like eloping lovers and my collected works were put to their best possible use and I loved you almost as much as I do now. Oh soon. Oh soon. Oh soon. Oh very soon, so very soon, AND NOW!"

And finally some letters trickled in. "My sweetheart, don't be disappointed and get the runaway blues because I'm coming to you . . . you'll have your Villefranche yet . . ." In hot and dusty London he carried me like a passport; mine was the only name he heard. "Your coolness and swift beauty is the Southwest wind which blows over the reeking asphalt."

He had somehow cleared his marriage with his father. On August 2, 1934, Malcolm joined me in New York.

Act Two

Who is the third who walks always beside you?
When I count, there are only you and I together
But when I look ahead up the white road
There is always another one walking beside you
Gliding wrapt in a brown mantle, hooded
I do not know whether a man or a woman
—But who is that on the other side of you?
—T.S. Eliot, "The Waste Land"

When Malcolm arrived in New York on August 2, 1934, mother and I were at the dock to meet him. He emerged from the *Aquitania* looking absolutely marvelous—trim, slender, totally handsome. Mother was captivated. He was the son she had never had and she greeted him with delight. Our reunion was brief, however—Malcolm was in his Melville period and had planned for us to sail at once for New Bedford, which he envisioned as a nineteenth-century whaling village.

At the ticket window, he absent-mindedly dropped his wallet containing our total worldly goods; recovering it, I was henceforth appointed Minister of Finance.

New Bedford depressed us both; in no way would it replace Villefranche, nor would we find an acceptable substitute till Martha's Vineyard where we at last made up for our arid weeks of separation. August 10 was a special night to remember. We yielded totally to each other and made of the date a talismanic reminder of all we owed to one another.

At Malc's suggestion, I had brought Van de Velde's *Ideal Marriage*. Our sun-filled days now became a smorgasbord of the untried as we experimented with its suggestions. Once, when we were prowling about Menemsha, Malc called to me, "I can hear your sex from here . . . it roars in the sunlight." I thought it a joyous line. He told me he'd brought the book to Jeakes House, where the Aikens lived when in Rye, and that it had provoked an alarmed outcry from Conrad: "For God's sake, don't let Jerry see it." (Poor Jerry, I thought smugly.)

Many mornings we wandered to the pier to watch newcomers disembark. I recall one hot and extremely aggravated priest fuming his way along the gangplank, and from somewhere the friendly hoot: "Take it easy, Reverend, you'll get your bowels in an uproar."

After ten days we moved on to Provincetown, a move which

acquainted me with another Malcolm-trait: rather than pack, he would discard everything except such notes as he had not "mislaid." In leaving France he'd abandoned even the handsome clothes with which he had arrived. Seeking, therefore, to defend his wardrobe, from that time forward it was I who packed.

At Provincetown we found a sunny cottage at 447 Commercial Road—two rooms, a tiny private beach, and a rear porch from which to watch the breakers. Many nights we swam nude. Here we worked seriously, acquired a few acquaintances, and had long engrossing conversations and one blowup. Malcolm worked on the short stories he had brought from Paris and started making notes for *In Ballast to the White Sea,* which in part explored his relationship with Nordahl Grieg, the Norwegian novelist, whom he had visited in Oslo in the summer of 1931. I was working up my own book, to be called *I'll See You in Paris.*

Our companions were generally the Blaus who ran the local bookstore during the summer. Through them, we attended one or two beach parties enlivened by a sprinkling of literary lights including Edmund Wilson and Mary Heaton Vorse. At these sunset gatherings there would be good talk, drinkable wine, and a generous overlay of gossip; yet, ever averse to coteries not of his election, Malcolm soon rejected our participation. In retrospect, I suppose we were absurd; I, growing embattled; he, vociferous. Reminding him that our vows were purely marital, I insisted they had not installed me in a cloister, at which his accusations became so heated I sought a tearful refuge on our beach. When I reentered the cottage, Malc was gone.

Later, among his papers, I found a letter to Tom Forman, written that clouded evening but not mailed: . . . this letter would advise Tom he was dead . . . he wished it clear I was in no way connected with his death . . . he'd been really happy with me and for a time had made me happy too . . . but it was hopeless. "I remain with a corpse, so that all that beauty we knew must pass in sable by . . . My ghost will protect you. Break my camp." Such letters were intended for me and were of only such moment.

That fall we returned to New York and leased a pleasant apartment at 99 Perry Street; it would not have occurred to us to look elsewhere than Greenwich Village.

New York, like Paris, is a walker's city, and we were tireless walkers. Living quite near the Hudson River, it was easy to stroll toward its docks chomping on pushcart hot dogs and potato pancakes, and pausing for Malc to note street signs, graffiti, or names of waterfront cafes. We usually wound up at the public library. Movies and theaters and restaurants were plentiful and cheap. On Malcolm's monthly stipend of 150 dollars, we were practically in Fat City, and I squirreled away a portion for "emergencies," such as the navy wool overcoat he bought on 14th Street that winter for 12 dollars.

In September, "Hotel Room in Chartres" appeared in *Story,* and shortly afterward we received our first invitation from Whit Burnett, its editor, to a "literary tea" to be held September 24 at the house of Charles Studin at 12 East 10 Street, New York. It was a party to launch a collection of Whit's short stories at which he was chief guest. He wanted us along, he said, "to meet some people." He also said that Malcolm, as a contributor to *Story*, was now eligible for its thousand-dollar contest in which he would like to see *Ultramarine* or his other novel entered.

We had been working hard on submissions, so far with no results. Malcolm was working mainly on short stories while I concentrated on *I'll See You in Paris,* though Malc's seas of symbolism befogged its introduction. (My main character was named Jill Firmin, and I later noted with some surprise Malcolm's adoption of her surname for his consul in *Under the Volcano.* Of further interest was the means of Yvonne's death—under a horse's hooves; for in my Paris book a character loosely based on Julian had been similarly slain by mounted police during the riots at the Place de la Concorde in 1934.)

En route to our second cocktail party at Charles Studin's, we stopped for cigarettes and I noticed an absolutely stunning girl accompanied by a tall and balding man. In a few minutes we ran into them again, this time at Studin's; the man was Donald Friede, of the publishing house Covici-Friede; the girl, his third wife, Anna. Theirs was a companionably open marriage. Anna was dating William Harlan Hale, whom she would later wed. An aspiring writer does not turn down a dinner invitation with a publisher. So, dining with Donald later, I found him colorful, a *fin-de-siècle* personality whose fund of literary anecdotes was boundless. During the evening a pass was subtly implied but, parried, was allowed to die. More to the point, he read my stories and approved of them.

Following the disaster of the diaries episode, I'd tried to discuss everything openly with Malcolm, so I now told him about the evening, admittedly enjoyable and promising, hopeful that he'd progressed beyond his early jealousy; and indeed he appeared to accept the dinner equably enough. But the next day brought a change; he first turned accusatory, then banged from the apartment.

When evening came and he still had not returned, I snacked at an automat and on re-entering the flat discovered one of Malc's notes. I could date whom I wished; men were plentiful and wealthy and good looking. To love me took no special aptitude for I was beautiful, but he did *really* love me . . .

The note left me abashed. I knew I had been dazzled by the evening; in Europe flirtations were light hearted, even casual, but flirting was a largely European skill. Not English, not American, and certainly not Malcolm's with his Nordic *angst*.

There followed more parties at Studin's, after one of which Malcolm received a note from Allan Seager of *Vanity Fair* inviting submission of light humorous pieces of not over 2,500 words. It was a nice note but fruitless. Malcolm did not write "light" or "humorous" pieces.

From Malcolm's parents, we continued to receive letters; those from his mother inevitably suggested one of those ladies played by Margaret Rutherford—warm-hearted, a little fusty around the edges, with just a dash of that bumbling eccentricity which has rendered so many Upholders of the Empire at once maddening and dear. Among the papers Malcolm left with mother, I found, years later, a letter from his father written around Thanksgiving of 1934. As usual, it was affectionate but carping. He had been glad that Malcolm and I were very happy but it seemed Malcolm's concern was only with himself. The past he discarded "as easily as a worn-out suit," and both his parents with it. It had been left to Arthur Lowry to patch up the disaster left behind in Paris where it appeared such damage had been visited upon 7, rue Antoine-Chantin that a lawsuit had resulted. Apart from such tasks and the monthly checks, Arthur had written, "I am of no account to you," and having dangled *Green Corners of the Earth* before his mother as a "sacred effort," a nice religious work just for her, Malcolm now announced that "having been dislocated, the book is, of course, shelved, which is a pity." What of their "wounded hearts?"

If Malc thought about his family at all, it could not have been often. He feared and respected Arthur. His mother, Evelyn was the recipient of "Mother dearest" letters from time to time, only at Arthur's insistence and to ensure that his stipend was not cut off. He and Stuart, his eldest brother and once his hero, had drifted apart; Wilfrid, long married, had likewise left home. Only Russell, with whom Malcolm had had a major disagreement before leaving England, remained unmarried and at home, kept on a low salary working at his father's office. When it came to writing to his mother, I was recruited, as was Margerie, my successor, in her turn.

As to the return ticket for the *Aquitania,* Arthur had made provisional arrangements with Cunard to substitute two third-class tickets on the *Berengaria,* sailing January 25 for Southampton. Malc had only to cable acceptance of the offer. But Malc never informed me of this due, no doubt, to the panoply of opportunities New York presented him. Though understandable, it proved an unfortunate decision.

At a party that fall, given by *Story* and Modern Library to promote "The Word," we reencountered the Blaus, whom we'd not seen since

Provincetown. Malcolm got stoned and they innocently accompanied us as we were leaving. There had been a dearth of food and three of us wanted to go somewhere for supper. One of us did not. And that one became obstreperous.

"Chatter! Babble! Chatter! Babble! Christ, I'm sick of it!" Malc shouted, throwing off Joe Blau's grasp with such force that both men staggered momentarily. "You piddling little bellboy people! Chatter and babble! Chatter and babble! Why don't you just GO AWAY?"

"Malcolm," I urged nervously. "You're making a scene. Please, Malcolm . . ." A small crowd had started to gather and I tried to take his arm.

He made a sweeping if unsteady gesture. "God damn it now, let go of me! And go to hell, all of you!" Lurching as though battling a gale, he struck off in the opposite direction.

The Blaus looked absolutely stunned. "What happened to him?" Joe demanded.

"The liquor hit him and he's drunk."

"Yes, well—I guess we'd better get on, too." And mumbling something vaguely apologetic, they beat a grateful, permanent retreat, for we never saw them again. Those who had stopped to stare at us began to drift away. I spent the night with my old theater friends Ted and Anne, still living in New York. Since it was hopeless to try to cope with Malcolm during his liquored rages, I had developed the protective response of absenting myself at the grimmest of such upheavals; not to lovers, as Conrad Aiken endlessly surmised, but through that instinct which leads us to avert our gaze from carnage.

When I returned to Perry Street next day, it was to find another of Malc's note's, this one both tender and remorseful. He was out looking for me. I had only to be away this long for him to realize how much he loved and needed me . . . the minutes were as wounded . . . he promised he would concentrate on work and help as he could with mine . . . he must be blind not to realize I was the finest thing in life . . .

But cocktail parties invariably meant binges, some worse than others and more lacerating. And one produced another note, which I found on my pillow when I returned from mother's:

> Jan, I need you so. I have gone to bed just thinking of you and your tenderness and loveliness, so that I could hardly close my eyes to this room where are the things you yourself touch and move about amongst like the person in the poem you liked. [Aiken's "Music I Heard," which so moved me, in my teens, I memorized it in memory of father.] It does not matter that I need you, but there is something in me so hellishly powerful it must matter to you, I know. I am no longer a writing-paper lover as you call me. And I have not been unfaithful to thee . . . in my or anybody else's fashion.
>
> I have straightened your bed tenderly but without conviction. It looks like the Red Sea. And I used your pillowcase. Come and say goodnight, Jani. Sleep well, my beloved.

Yet before the year was out we had a worse quarrel over Malcolm's drunkenness, and this time it was he who removed himself to mother's. His condition must have been disillusionment aplenty, but unable to let bad enough alone, he sought to win her sympathy by attacking me and at this her patience snapped.

"You're speaking of my daughter, Malcolm Lowry," she told him furiously. "Neither you nor anybody—*do you understand me?*—speaks to me like that about my child." She continued to feed and shelter him, and she sobered him up to boot, but she never really forgave him although the ultimate disintegration of our marriage saddened her greatly. She had had such hopes for us.

During that stay, Malc wrote a will leaving me his books, car, and income, for which he wished me to go to Liverpool to arrange with his family. He wished them to treat me as a daughter, allowing me all the freedom I wished. He wanted me to try to make something out of the rough notes for his novel along the lines he had discussed with me from time to time, and if necessary to consult with John Davenport about it. He wanted me to see that his play was produced and his short stories were published. While in Europe he wished me to visit Nordahl Grieg, and he willed the photograph of himself as a child to *his* mother and all income from his posthumous works to *my* mother. This was one of many subsequent "wills," all of which were destroyed.

After each of his binges he was usually apologetic and embarrassed, but generally able to obliterate rapidly the more acrid memories. And because he had rendered all other men pallid by comparison I continued to adjust, mindful by now of how much I had come to love him.

∾   ∾   ∾

Nineteen thirty-five dawned quietly. By and large it would be our best year. We'd decided to complete a body of work for Malcolm and then travel, possibly to South America where Malcolm was eager to visit Lake Titicaca and Tierra del Fuego, names which enchanted him.

To expedite these plans, I set aside my book to type his manuscripts; he had special hopes for "Bulls of the Resurrection" and "A Goddam Funny Ship." Right off the bat, however, we encountered problems with the latter . . . the title was considered blasphemous. To the suggestion that he call it "A Doggone Funny Ship," he reacted coldly, while the further proposal "A Goldarn Funny Ship," provoked disgusted mirth.

Around this time he told me of a particularly distressing episode to which he ascribed much of the guilt which haunted him, its prologue a childhood memory of a pet rabbit given to him when he was eight years old, on which he'd either stepped or fallen, breaking its back so that it had to be destroyed. He had been inconsolable.

To this childhood grief he credited his conviction that he would probably destroy whatever he most loved, and he described to me the death of a fellow student at Cambridge for which he felt himself responsible. As he related it, he and his friend Paul had been drinking

heavily and the talk had turned to suicide, to which Paul felt driven for
reasons Malcolm did not specify. Malcolm was sure, however, that he'd
egged Paul on, even accompanying him to his room and helping jam
papers and rags around the window frame; he was sure, too, his final
words had been "Now do it!"

Whether true or not, Paul was found dead the next morning,
though Malcolm's assumption of guilt remains questionable. His imagination embroidered so many of his relationships, it is impossible at this
date to determine which were accurate; for to at least some degree he
embellished most of them.

The morbidity of this tale is mirrored in much of what he wrote,
especially *In Ballast to the White Sea,* which contains a virtually
identical episode save that Paul has become the protagonist's brother,
Tor, and both characters, in effect, were Malc himself.

In March of 1935 I was hospitalized for ten days. During one of our
impassioned couplings, Malcolm had bitten me on my breast and the
wound had become abscessed. I waited for it to surface and become
treatable; when it didn't, I entered St. Vincent's Hospital and became
a patient in Ward B, which was a world in miniature. After ten days my
breast had healed sufficiently to permit my departure, but Malcolm
failed to retrieve his lady love. No one could locate him. Unescorted, I
returned to Perry Street to discover the door ajar and both Malcolm and
my North African silver bracelets gone. Because they'd been evocative
of the *souks* in which I'd bargained for them and of my carefree
wanderings, I mourned them doubly. I discovered later that Malc had
gone off on one of his usual binges and had probably left the door of the
apartment open, inviting anyone to enter. I didn't accuse him of this or
of having neglected me in the hospital, and we managed to carry on as
if nothing had happened.

∽   ∽   ∽

Early in 1935 we decided it was time for a change and temporarily
moved to mother's until our plans could coalesce. There was work to

complete and circulate and so, as a "purely temporary" measure, we then put up at the Hotel Somerset on 47th Street. Its location proved ideal; close by were subways and buses, movies and theaters, cafes and automats, and Central Park. And above all, of course, the library.

Our hotel was good to us, even providing without charge, as it became available, a vacant room which could be used as an office. I bought a small hot plate—which took care of breakfast there. Gradually, the few weeks we had planned to spend there lengthened until we had been there one year. That period of 1935 was the gentlest of our marriage. We were most productive; we were both working; we had settled down to a good writing routine—we got along very well together—there was trust, there was complete communication at all levels, whether writing or talking. Malc was busy with his agent; I typed his work and likewise my own. We went constantly to theaters and to movies, restaurants were inexpensive. More and more we "lived" at the New York Public Library and visited Central Park, a delight, for everything we needed was close to the Somerset.

It is sad to realize that Central Park became synonymous with crime. For us it was a garden where we could roam for hours; where in the hot soft summer nights we'd stroll beside the lake and feel refreshed; and where we'd visit our pet duck—a duckling really, with a sweetly foolish topknot, who inevitably became one of our many symbols. Our notes scheduling rendezvous would often close, "I'll meet you in the Park by the little duck."

At first Malc was working on producing short stories for *So We Live Forever Taking Leave,* which he had begun in Paris, and was trying to get published. Though not a teller of tales like Somerset Maugham, his characters came from within, always a voyage, an interior voyage. But at the Somerset *In Ballast to the White Sea* mainly engrossed him.

I had returned from Europe with two books in mind. One was to be called *Vagabondage,* which would be the story of my travels; the other would be called *I'll See You in Paris.* Malcolm was always involved with symbols, and I got the virus. So when I started an outline of *I'll See You in Paris,* it became so convoluted with the number three and its relationship to my characters that it grew to close on 200 pages. I showed it to one editor, but the number three did me in.

One day the press headlined a terrible catastrophe in the coal mines in Pécs, where Erszi lived and which I'd explored when visiting her in 1933. The report so horrified me that I began to gather whatever material I could find with the intention of basing a story on the tragedy. All but living at the library, it became an obsession, and I sent pages of questions to Erszi for clarification. On May 23, 1935, Malc and I set out to hitch-hike to Pennsylvania to get some working knowledge of a coal mine.

I'd written the Hudson Coal Company of Scranton, and they'd extended invitations to us both. By the time we left New York, I was reasonably conversant with much of Hungary's post–World War I history: the regimes of Count Michael Karolyi and of Bela Kun, of the fascistic Admiral Horthy and Julius Gomboes (who together were responsible for the infamous White Terror which, from its onset and at their instigation, tortured and murdered over 200,000 Jews and dissidents, and from 1921 until the onslaught of the Nazi hordes was known as the worst dictatorship in Europe). It was no doubt due to my involvement with this project—never, alas, completed—that I found myself dubbed "a Socialist writer," or, in England, among those fastidiously obsessed with bloodlines, "a Jewish Socialist writer." Uninvolved as I was, however, on a deeper level they did me too much honor.

Hitch-hiking was fun, for it was not yet dangerous to seek rides or to offer them and our highway hosts seemed grateful for company. We spent several days at the mine while I took pages of notes and Malc made sketches to accompany them, and on returning to New York we received a long letter thanking us for our visit and inviting us to return at any time. (We had shamelessly told them we were from the *New York Times*.)

Meantime, Harold Matson had been circulating Malcolm's stories and a draft of *In Ballast,* as well as *Ultramarine* with which a disturbing issue suddenly erupted: Burton Rascoe, a Random House editor, discovered what he called major plagiarisms from *American Caravan*, an anthology to which he had contributed in 1928. This could indeed be serious, and Malcolm sought to defuse the problem, drafting and redrafting a letter of explanation. (How worried he was is apparent in one of the rough drafts, for in several margins is penciled "Help me, O.C."; this, by way of a prayer to the old captain with whom, as he'd informed me in Paris, his sister-in-law Margo communicated through her Ouija board. It also suggests Malc felt he could now approach the friendly shade *sans* intermediary.)

In his letter he made these points: While admitting there was a case for claiming plagiarism, he insisted it was a minor one, no more than a few paragraphs; though even so, he demanded an apology. His motives, however, had been honest, as he hoped to make quite clear. The passages had been adapted at "second hand"—he'd been eighteen at the time and "cooked to the crow's nest," i.e., drunk. It was possible they had been jotted down in the course of a seminar on the interior monologue while he was studying with Conrad Aiken. Or, if not there, the quotation may have been included in a friend's correspondence; it was at this time *Ultramarine* was taking form, and the passage might have occurred to him as being a "design-governing posture" for a section of the book. As originally written, he could vouch for there having been no plagiarism, but—a publisher having lost that version— he'd been unable to find copies for three of the lost chapters and had to reconstruct them from such notes as he could find. That the offending quotation may have been, all unconsciously, included was just possible since at this time he was "perpetually pie-eyed."

His explanation may have been accepted for we heard little more about it, though there were no takers for the book, and Malc now pinned his hopes upon *In Ballast*. Some 265 pages of *In Ballast* still survive in carbon. The book would end with the cry which epitomized those nightmare visions Malc both fled and craved: *"My God! What shall I do without my misery?"*

And thus 1935 passed, industrious and optimistic, with increasing tranquillity, only minor blowups, and the growing conviction that our marriage had finally achieved a solid base. We sensed in one another an increased purpose and an earned maturity. No longer did we seem that stormy disparate couple who had married almost haphazardly.

More and more I realized how Malc had altered me. Trained in the theater, I was accustomed to casual profanity, but Malc possessed the salty repertoire of a sailor, a ripeness of expression rivaling the Elizabethans (to whose period I felt he most belonged), and this soon flavored my own speech as well.

Of greater importance was his political awareness. Mother and Ted and Eldon had been devout Republicans and I had parroted them. Neither an activist nor one to man the barricades, Malc nonetheless educated me in the need to assess political jargon. *"Don't listen to what they say: watch what they do."* With Hitler and Mussolini swelling like abscesses upon Europe's body amid a worldwide ferment, by his example and his precepts Malc made of me a life-long liberal.

In yet another vein, he opened the esoteric: yoga, Ouspensky, Mme. Blavatsky. Though then inclined to denigrate the mystical, I at least became aware of these philosophies and would pursue some later. Also, Malcolm expanded my own outlook and interpretation of events. I had arrived in Europe imbued with mother's antiliberal assessments. Malcolm reversed these, broadened my outlook, and, as it were, re-educated me. Also he introduced me to such philosophical and literary influences as Swedenborg, Havelock Ellis, and Charles Fort among many others.

In 1936 our marriage took its most unhealthy turn. I wrote later about that fateful disintegrating spring:

We had been living at the Hotel Somerset for almost a year when we met Tony Valleton, who was tall and thin, a trifle stoop-shouldered and resolutely dedicated to the more bizarre legends of Alistair Crowley, of the young Aubrey Beardsley, of Lord Alfred Douglas, and Oscar Wilde. And André Gide.

We met him at a gin party which was at once a heritage from and an echo of the '20s. It was held in a cluttered dreary house in a

cluttered dreary town out on Long Island which belonged to a
Trinidadian writer named Martin to whom we had been introduced
by Waldo Frank; and Malcolm and I had gone there for a weekend
of what my memory retains mainly as a series of Grand Guignol
montages set against a background of incessant chatter which might
have been the amplified shrilling of a horde of locusts.

Everyone drank ceaselessly. There were loud arguments about
Fascism and Nazism and the responsibilities of the artist as a committed commentator versus the strict need to remain aloof and get on
with it. Inevitably there followed fights and tears and drunken
posturings, and the room, brown, with tattery orphaned furnishings,
seemed to creak like a battered barquentine beneath the assaults.

Martin's wife was away for the weekend with her music teacher,
but his mistress, a reddish woman who explained that she taught
Drawing I, eddied about mutely, tidying, collecting glasses and
emptying bottles with the silent dedication of a nun.

Malc was quickly engulfed by a brunette with much hair, who
wore a Joseph's coat of a garment with bits and tags of floating fabric,
who wove herself about him like a living tapestry. Her name was Nina
and when she smiled up at me she seemed to have four sets of teeth—
all serrate.

About a week after this hapless shindig, Malcolm decided he
needed a separate room; we had worked practically in each other's
pockets since moving to the Somerset. After some searching, I located
two small rooms at the Gotham House on East 86 Street and we moved
there in early May. It was during this period that Tony and Martin and
Malcolm and I, with various others, took to visiting Harlem. On one
such night when Tony stopped by for us, he seized on a hat which
boasted a long French veil of dark blue silk—(Malc called it my "woman
of mystery" hat) and insisted that I wear it.

"Voila! C'est Madame Chose et je suis son maquereau!"

On the uptown bus Malcolm was definitely not amused at the curious
glances attending Madame Chose in her enormous veil. We were en route

to a party at the Harlem apartment of Norman Macleod, the poet. Tony, as usual, became an instant star: possessor of a precise and poisoned wit, his fund of anecdotes was brazen and outrageous. I knew he was attracted to Malcolm—he'd made no secret of it—but though Malc and I had faced varying crises during the previous two years, the preference of homosex- uality was not among them. That Tony might disrupt the tenor of our lives seemed then unthinkable. Yet during that evening, maliciously encouraged by the hovering Tony, Malc broadcast the most private entries from my European journals. I broke apart and fled.

For the next two nights he did not come home at all, though he phoned once to say he was at Tony's, his speech so indistinct and blurred that I hung up on him. The following evening when I returned to the Gotham House, I was informed with quiet relish by the elevator man—who could well have served as caretaker at a charnel house—that my husband had moved out. "Came with another gentleman, he did, and took away all his things. He left this for you."

"This" was an envelope of questionable cleanliness, my name printed on it in block letters. Mutely, I took it. The elevator cables creaked as the old man and the old machine sighed downward and I entered my horrid room.

Malc's note was scrawled in pencil on yellow blotting paper in large and careless letters. For my sake, he was moving out. His novel had been accepted and the advance would keep him going for a month. If I needed anything, including money, he could be contacted at an address on MacDougal Street.

Could it actually be Malcolm who had written this brief and icy note? I read and reread the few lines, too stunned to grasp what had befallen us. The bitterness and anger of the recent days were stripped away as the ground on which I'd stood now flung me into space.

To Malc I wrote a protest and a prayer, a cry for help. When I alighted from the bus at Washington Square, I walked in the wrong direction and for the life of me couldn't remember where MacDougal Street turned off. Tension clouded my wits. A man delivering a parcel eventually directed me.

But I was going to do the wrong thing, say the wrong thing, and I knew it. I also knew that the sunlight, the too-vivid lipstick against the pallor of my face, the black beret, and the suit—would all have given to me a hard look. It was the look I called my "mask of self-defense." Very early, around thirteen or fourteen, this defensive mask had settled about my lips and eyes. A nervous, unsure, and self-conscious adolescent, I unconsciously flexed my facial muscles from sheer fright when I confronted strangers. I never wore the look with intimates, but it was often my shield against the world and I knew I wore it now. (Oddly enough, I had not needed it in Europe.)

At 138 MacDougal Street a sign proclaimed "Angelina's" and below, in small letters, "Rooms." At the head of the stairs I came face to face with a mountainous blowsy woman—Angelina herself. "I'm Mrs. Lowry. I'm here to see my husband. Which room is his?"

"He's asleep," said Angelina through tight lips.

"That's wasn't what I asked you. Where's his room?"

"It's upstairs but you can't disturb him now."

I was back in Paris with the concierges. I'm small but my voice can be authoritative. It was authoritative now. The bulky form gave way reluctantly, and I pushed past her and ran on up the stairs. On the top floor I found a bare landing with several padlocked rooms. A door at the far end of the hall stood partly open and I could see Malc's suitcase on a chair.

He was in bed. As I neared him, I was struck by a peculiar, cloying odor which, somewhere in memory, I'd once known. When Malc saw me he rolled over so that his back was toward me. I dropped my purse and leaned across the rumpled bedclothes to put my arms about him. I dared not cry: he might retreat beyond any hope of contact. He lay taut and watchful though presently a small sound escaped him and I saw his cheek was damp. "Oh, Janl . . ."

"Oh, Malcolm, oh my darling, what has happened to us?"

He only murmured as before, "Oh Janl, Janl . . ."

The strange odor assailed me afresh, pungent, disquieting, and once again memory struggled just beyond recognition. He was very flushed, wearing a cheap white shirt I'd never seen, and his hair was thickly oiled. I passed my hand through it to stroke it and an oily scent clung to my fingertips. "I've missed you so. Why did you leave like that?"

But he only shook his head, and when I tried to turn him toward me, he resisted. It was a tawdry drama and all of it unreal: a garret with its sloping ceiling; a broken windowpane, patched hopefully; the barren floor; one small scarred table; two spent chairs. I knew well that the offer of a drink would accomplish more than any plea or argument but that first one inevitably multiplied until all count was lost. So had we landed here.

Abruptly the odor which emanated from him, drenching the room, grew recognizable: it was the odor of embalming fluid, that sweet and sickly smell of dissolution, and I had smelled it years before when my father died—first in the mortuary and again at his services at the Masonic Temple. What was it called? Formaldehyde? Paraldehyde? And why did I smell it here?

I moved to the patched window and stared out. At Washington Square, the trees and benches would be bathed in sunlight. Below, a knot of children struggled: was it a game? But their voices rising toward me shrilled with spite. The bedsprings creaked, and when I turned, Malcolm was facing me.

"You look very charming," he said, almost humbly. "But can't you understand? I'm tired. I want to sleep. I just want to be left alone. You can come back later," he added hopefully.

With all our lives at stake? To be informed that Malcolm had gone out? That Tony had collected him? I shook my head.

"For God's sake, Jan! I'm being reasonable!" But we were each imprisoned in our private pain. Mechanically I picked up his tweed jacket off the floor and shook it, but as I bent to retrieve his trousers, he cried sharply, "Please let my things alone!"

I dropped the jacket across a chair. "Malc, I can't live with this, losing you, doing absolutely nothing."

He pushed the covers away and began rubbing at his face. "All right, all right, I'm getting up," he said, and padded across the hall to the bathroom in his socks.

"Let's walk over to our old pier," I suggested, cautiously. "The one nearer the Savannah Line, remember?"

"I remember old men fishing through trap-holes. And river boats."

At West Street we turned, passing small bars and waterfront cafes, but the entrance to our pier was boarded up. Only a disinterested watchman guarded it; it had been declared unsafe. We were badly shaken: it had been another of our symbols.

"I wonder if our little duck still has his topknot," Malcolm said. "Those chaps who fished here—it was someplace for them to go . . . "At Perry Street he leaned against the railing. "Look here, Jan, be reasonable. We can't just go on walking—I'm all in. I could meet you for lunch later. Why don't you go off by yourself for an hour or two?"

"But we haven't settled anything at all."

"I have to be alone!" He almost shouted it.

Marriage had buried pride. Unable to postpone the issue any longer, I sank down on the steps of our old building. "Malcolm, does Tony mean anything to you really? You spent two nights with him. Was it because of him you left that way? I have to know."

He banged an open palm against the railing. "For God's sake quit harping on that theme. You ought to have more sense. Besides," he added presently, "there's something else . . . I guess I'll have to tell you."

I tried to interlink his fingers with my own but his would not respond.

"It was those nights with Tony . . ." As I watched his face, turned inward and remote, I thought, "*This is a deathwatch.*"

"We were so drunk those two nights, both of us, I haven't the slightest memory—only glimpses—Harlem and bits like that. But the truth is, he's under doctor's care—still getting treatment, that is, for what it's worth."

Now, finally, he looked at me directly. "And I was in his room and used his things. And Jan, God help us both, I can't remember anything that may have happened there."

I forced a prolonged breath. Even the word syphilis had held pure horror for him, fathering his prolonged virginity. "But Malcolm, maybe nothing happened. Couldn't you see a doctor right away, make sure? And Malc, if we're together . . ."

He shook his head. "You can't understand the way I feel, not about this. It may take months to know I'm safe again. And every time we quarreled, you'd throw it back at me."

"Oh Malc, you know I wouldn't."

He rose with finality, pulling me up with him. "You mean well, Starkey, I know that, but you're being no more reasonable than when we started out. And now I really have to go."

At Greenwich Avenue we paused. I put my hands on his and leaned my face for a moment against his chest. "You'll be careful? You will be careful? Please?"

"I'll call you," he said. "Soon." His lips brushed my hair, and with a final pressure of my hands, he walked rapidly in the direction from which we'd come like a man who is late for an appointment.

Though I now had to find work, in the ensuing days I was turned down for Editorial Assistant; rejected as Photographer's Receptionist; and rebuffed by Ma Bell, whose minions disapproved of the "separated" I'd jotted alongside "marital status."

Unprepared for such starchy morality as a prerequisite for uttering "Number, please?" I turned my attention to the nonjudgmental: mail, including a note from Donald Friede, living now in Hollywood. "You promised to keep in touch with me, and keep me posted about your work. You know that I think that with proper development you can be a fine writer. And how long is it now since I heard from you? And what have you done about sending me your work? . . . Now do write and send some samples of what you're doing . . . I may be able to be of more help to you than you seem to think . . ."

Because of Malc, I had avoided Donald; his letter gave me hope, but only momentarily. What I wanted most of all was that life with Malcolm which had just begun to find its footing. There was yet worse to come.

Through the intervention of Erik Estorick, another writer we had also met through Waldo Frank, Malc entered Bellevue Hospital. Estorick and I knew little of one another, his involvement being primarily with Malcolm, but I saw no reason then to question his conclusion that Malc required therapy. I'd been advised that for this period I should maintain my distance; Malc desperately needed help and his treatment must be given every chance. Our futures and our marriage were on hold.

Through Ted and Anne I located a pleasant small apartment at 12 West 68th Street, off Central Park West. My windows overlooked the interiors of vast two-storied studios which, rightly or wrongly, I believed those of the Hotel des Artistes. From time to time, remote and dispossessed, through the windows I'd watch gatherings therein as though watching theaters. And before taking possession of my new small home, I found a job: I became a taxi dancer.

"Look, Jan, that's the sign I was telling you about." Anne pointed across the street where, in colored lights THE VARSITY blinked on and off. Below it streamed a banner: WANTED: HOSTESSES!

"But why is that always there? Don't any of the girls stay on?"

Teddy looked smug. "After they break them in, they ship them to Buenos Aires."

"Oh darling, don't be such an ass! They probably move on to someplace else."

He eyed us mischievously. "I dare you, both of you, to ask for jobs. You could say you worked in London, make up anything."

"Come off it, Ted." Depression had made me irritable.

"Well, why not? You're the writer after all. Aren't you the least bit curious?"

"Not about that I'm not. Besides, I'm a rotten dancer."

"I don't mean apply seriously, for God's sake! Just see if they'd even take you. I'd hardly describe you two as tarty types."

"We *could* just take a look," Anne said. "We've done crazy things before."

We had, too. One weekend, when they were broke, Anne and I had carted boxes of Teddy's hats through Brooklyn and peddled them door to door— "a buck apiece." We'd managed to sell eight. And when I was eighteen, I'd written a vaudeville sketch which we'd called "The Hat

Shop" and managed to book it into a Loew's theater in the Bronx. Not wishing to tarnish my "literary' name" I'd called myself Judith Grant. Eldon came to see us and thought the skit was funny. Everyone else, however, had been stunned and we were promptly canceled. I still recall the anguish in the booking agent's voice: "But Miss Grant, what on earth has *happened*."

"Well, make up your mind," Ted said impatiently. "We can't stand here all night."

Remembering how I'd wandered through the deserts of North Africa yet refused an offer to tour with the Hungarians, I warned myself that timidity was fatal to experience. Besides, there would be two of us: it was easier to be reckless when accompanied.

Immersed in *Billboard*, Teddy waited at a newsstand. "That wasn't long. What did they have to say?"

"We're in. They hired us both. We start on Monday."

He looked taken aback. "They must be desperate. What's the place like inside?"

"Not too bad. Smallish. The manager seems nice. And that reminds me—I'm going to need a gown."

He replaced *Billboard* and bought a *Daily News*. "You are planning to make this into your life's work?"

"Maybe a week or so. What do you say, Jan?"

I temporized. "A day or two perhaps. It could prove interesting."

"Lady Lowry, the dance-hall babe," Ted jeered. "I'm betting you'll both be running home before the first night's over."

"You could be there to act as our protector."

"Not me," he said, indifferent alike to grammar and to gallantry. "I'm not watching you make idiots of yourselves. I'll meet you after work. And now if you two dance-hall queens want to stand here all night discussing your careers, go right ahead. I'm going to take a walk." And he set off at a brisk clip, inexplicably ruffled. Clearly, our unexpected hiring on was bothering him.

Prior to 1926, dance-halls were unlicensed. In 1931, all licenses were transferred to the Police Department. A series of articles with photos by Mignonne Bushel in the early thirties resulted in the elimination of the lovebooths. The current guidelines, few and basic, were not to be ignored. Those customers who'd paid to sit at the tables were surprised to learn they'd paid to sit alone, totally separated from their hostesses by railings; to perch on a railing meant risking a police record. Other taboos included touching a seated customer, accompanying him to the bar or the cashier's cage, accepting money, kissing while dancing, and failing to split all tips with management. Though forbidden to leave the hall with a customer or to meet him in front of it, a hostess could nonetheless be "bought out" for the hours remaining in her shift.

Most girls went into taxi dancing as a means of tiding themselves over and remained only a few months. It was the exception who practiced prostitution or took dope. To be drunk was to be fired immediately. Some girls arrived via burlesque; some were married, perhaps with children; a few were well educated. There were mothers who introduced their daughters to the life, girls who'd worked 18 or more years, and girls who married customers. Among the latter, as I learned years later, would be Anne.

For the first week only, we were guaranteed ten dollars. The dressing room, though tattier, was not unlike those I'd known in theaters. Besides Julie, the attendant, a Mrs. Bank popped in to sell gowns, lingerie, and G-strings. Her counterpart was the men's room attendant who dispensed booze and condoms.

For our first night I was decked out in my European eggshell satin; Anne, in a new black lace with flashing rhinestone straps: Teddy had done us proud. Our voices gave us away—hers surprisingly rich and husky for her size; mine, between theater training and my years with Malcolm, equally low, with more than a trace of England. For reassurance, we stood together behind the mandatory railing. Before long we were approached by a scruffy character who all but recoiled at our first words: "Hush! Edjicated Janes!" he snorted, vanishing.

Our next nonconquest was a major who offered twenty-five dollars if we would sit in a bus in a Hoboken garage. We didn't bother to ask why.

Almost without exception, the girls we worked with saw their lives as pages from *True Story* and *True Romance*. Immature, unrealistic, incurably sentimental, they eternally awaited Romeos, wealthy and generous, who could shower them with luxuries and ennoble them with passion. Meantime, they readily convinced themselves that every man fell victim to their charms. "He's crazy about me," was a common boast.

Our mixed bag of customers expanded. A pleasant-faced florist danced with me through three sets of tickets and later sent me gardenias. Anne met a pilot with a frolicsome sense of humor. Inevitably there were college boys who doled out their tickets one at a time, seeking hopefully those girls who could fly with them to hotels. We made not quite three dollars apiece on that first night.

Teddy met us at closing, four A.M., and we breakfasted on eggs, bacon, and hash browns in those glorious days before "thou shall set no cholesterol before thee" became, as it were, the eleventh commandment.

When I discovered that Malcolm was in Bellevue Hospital *psychiatric* ward being treated for *alcoholism,* I immediately went to see him. I don't know what sort of reputation Bellevue presently enjoys, but at that time the very name, for many, conjured up scenes from Bedlam. My visit there with Malc was unforgettable.

He had been in the hospital for little more than a week. However, his color precisely echoed the ashen hue of his worn hospital robe, and he appeared so shaky, so pitiably vulnerable, it was a moment before either of us could speak. Had Goya, Daumier, and Georg Grosz combined their bitterest talents, I thought, they could hardly have envisioned worse.

He gripped his black and white exercise book, filled as it was with the copious and nearly illegible notes which were to form the basis for *The Last Address* (later called *Lunar Caustic*). Even apart from his shakiness and pallor there was a further issue to disturb us both: how might this record of confinement in a psychiatric ward, and in Bellevue of all places, affect the imminent extension of his visa? Concerned now for our futures, I set the wheels for his release in motion and he was soon out.

He located a room at 24 West 71st Street, not far from my own, and we met frequently, our meetings poignant. One day he taught me a new song from England, "These Foolish Things"—haunting in melody, its wistful lyrics might have been composed especially for us.

He was again at work on *In Ballast* while I engulfed myself in notes about the dance-hall, pages of episodes, pages of characters. I'd made Malc aware of my activities, though not where I was working lest he burst into the Varsity while drunk. We had breakfast together from time to time; we lunched together occasionally, saw movies, took long walks, went to Central Park. Sometimes he would leave notes for me in carefully polished prose, which he often worked up through as many as three drafts. Some years later, reminiscing, I wrote:

> The radio is playing Gershwin's "Summertime," and the gentle, evocative music calls up that oddly innocent and tawdry era of 1935 when Malc and I saw *Porgy and Bess* and wandered New York, and loved, or thought we loved . . . Lost days seem always days of light and tenderness. Our youth, remembered, appears luminous; our follies, touching; and we see ourselves part Don Quixote and part Alice. The clumsiness, the waste, the cruelties—these we submerge and cover, meticulous as cats.
>
> So now, remembering the summer of 1936 my mind closes itself to bestiality and purges and summons instead the hot late New York nights—moist, airless and provocative—and I remember Malc . . . the sea-blue eyes, the shock of light brown hair, the lovely lovely voice, the closeness I have never known with anyone and distances which were to grow past bridging. Poignance. Destruction. Need and desperation. Losing and finding. Losing and finding . . . . Losing.
>
> And the hot steaming New York nights like no nights anywhere, in which we wandered, Malcolm and I, two figures out of Dante, unable to let go, unable to hold on . . .
>
> "These Foolish Things,"—Malc sang it to me, taught it to me on our walks . . . our song.

Jan as a child with her mother, 1911

Malcolm, Paris, 1934

Jan at a café in Belgium, 1933

Jan (with friend, Ilse Koldeman) in Berlin, 1933

Malcolm with Tom Foreman, North Wales, 1933

Jan in the south of France, during her tour of Europe, 1934

Malcolm at Fontenoy-aux-Roses just outside Paris, 1934

Jan on board the *Ile de France* bound for New York, May 1934

Malcolm with Mrs. Emily van der Heim, on Long Island,
shortly after his arrival in the USA, 1934

Malcolm, New York, 1934/5

The villa at Calle Humboldt 62 in Cuernnavaca

(Next page) The veranda of Calle Humboldt 62, describe◄
such disparaging terms by Arthur Calder-Mars

Malcolm and the Mexican guide who took the Lowrys to see a brothel in Oaxaca

Jan and Malcolm in a happy mood at Calle Humboldt

Jan at her apartment in Los Angeles after leaving Malcolm in Mexico

Jan in Los Angeles

Jan, in her later travels, in Haiti

Jan, on her return to Mexico in the early 1940s

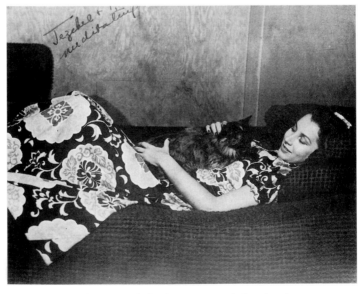

Jan and her cat Jezebel at her apartment in Los Angeles

❧ ❧ ❧

I was beginning to understand why so many girls returned to dance-hall life after exploring other fields. There was the approximation of allure: dressing each night in evening gowns, however tatty; the charade of being chosen, even for one ticket; the teasing challenge of ever-varying partners; the fillip of danger (girls had been beaten up); but perhaps most of all, that camaraderie which must infuse prison life, brothels, and army camps, crowding out memory. Girls came and went, but apart from surface differences, what they all sought was that spangled close-up of romantic love. The heat in the dressing-room, in those pre-air-conditioning days, was unbearable. Sweat poured off the girls' legs. When they sat on the benches, they pulled their skirts high; on the dance floor, giant fans had been installed and many of the girls caught colds.

The philosophy was cynical but verified: "Never go to a policeman when you're in trouble or a man is following you; when he hears you're a dance-hall dame he'll let the guy go and run you in for sure."

The customers were as varied as the girls. Horsejoe, from Montebello, who became enraged when overcharged one ticket; Max who told long stories about his shiksa girls and later took pretty Peggy to Lake George; Peter who had been badly injured in a rodeo but was returning to Montana anyway; the German, with a single ticket, attempting to fondle the breasts of any girl within reach; the gangster who bought Annette out every Wednesday, she all the while piously proclaiming her strict virtue; the degenerate, Harry, who was said to drink girls' urine but was otherwise considered harmless.

Anne acquired Dick, a detective, who dated and fell in love with her. (Less happily, she'd attracted a priapist she dubbed Jimmy Durante.) When the son of a New Jersey police chief sought, as they say, her hand, she was mercilessly kidded about her fatal power over lawmen.

One of my customers was an Australian journalist who wore a monocle and was a lot of fun. One dawn we took a bus ride to the Battery, and he presented me with a copy of Woolcott's "While Rome Burns."

With Pierre I spoke French; he came from Martinique and told wonderfully Marius stories with their Marseilles background. There was a Belgian—more chance to practice French. There was Boggy Powers, a small-time hoodlum, who was terribly impressed by my accent and told me I had "class." He wanted to set me up in an apartment but was good humored about it when I laughed at him. There was a Hungarian who gave *me* dancing lessons, and Jack who wrote to me from college, and a boy from Annapolis who invited me to the forthcoming prom.

And there was Peak.

It was Peak who remained my friend for many years, and one of my few confidants, though about him I knew almost nothing. Small, slim, neat, possibly in his thirties, he worked in a bookstore. He was never my customer for he danced with many girls, but he became my friend. His was a totally metaphysical turn of mind, totally nonjudgmental, and though he preached nothing, he came as close to the embodiment of goodness as I have ever known. He would help anyone; he condemned nobody; he saw through superficialities and possessed an asexual quality without the bindings of repression. I once read in a book by Muriel Rukeyser about Willard Gibbs that Gibbs was composed of science and of self till ultimately he threw the self away. That, too, was Peak: he had thrown the self away.

I introduced him to Malcolm who persisted in referring to him in letters as "Peke" and was, as always, convinced that any of my friends diminished *us*. Still, he minded Peak less than most. Peak, for his part, admired Malc enormously, both as man and talent. He was the one person to whom I could pour out my problems from Mexico and for some time thereafter. For years he sent me Christmas cards from a YMCA in Philadelphia; a few years back they stopped. Though we had long since ceased any true communication, I felt my world diminished.

I was now getting by solely on my dance-hall earnings, of between 18 and 22 dollars per week. Still in possession of a small sum I'd saved over the past two years, I was determined it must see us through to Mexico, which had replaced South America in our plans. Therefore when Malcolm, sole recipient now of his allowance, sought to "borrow" from me, I turned him down and, of course, a spat ensued. In truth, throughout this period I was reliving more and more our London days when his emotional demands had so exhausted me. And I suppose that, just as in London, a part of me was pulling back and he recognized this.

So, though we walked often in the park and revisited our now monumental duck, and found a small cat, quietly neatening, our unacknowledged tug of war continued. Often I wondered: did I know Malc at all? Or would I ever know him?

Then came the day when Conrad Aiken reappeared. Like much of what he wrote about us, the account of our dinner which he gave in *Ushant* is vintage nonsense. Malc must have contributed to it by assuring him Harper had taken his novel (as yet unfinished), and that it would be out in January; also that *Story* was featuring his (unwritten) novelette on Bellevue, "to be out next month." Neither of these assurances possessed a word of truth, nor does Aiken's depiction of a "*quondam* sweetheart" assuring Malc they had "something in common" and cadging drinks.

The tale is simpler: we'd met Ray, a young novelist, at a cocktail party. After Malc and I separated, I had run into Ray at the library and we had dined together. When he promised me a copy of his book, I'd told him where we usually dined and suggested he drop by and say hello to Malc, whereby, all innocently, he became enmeshed in the slithering skein Aiken forever wove, depicting me as wanton as Messalina and as pitiless as Circe (and, of course, high-heeled).

In later years, noting Ray's growing movie credits, I'd recall a decent, kind, white-blond young man who had offered friendship when I'd needed it but who remained stolidly pedestrian when compared with Malc. Though I no longer remember their many names, I was a faithful follower of his successes for some years till his fantasies were replaced by a newer genre.

I was now 25. On Malcolm's twenty-seventh birthday, Spain erupted into civil war. We grieved for the republican government, which had had no chance, but we remained uninvolved. It was one thing to cheer Roosevelt and to boo Hitler, but we were not activists, we were liberals—that breed which radio and newspaper columnist Walter Winchell once described as having "both feet firmly planted in the sky."

One letter I received from Malcolm after our temporary separation reveals careful reworking and development of ideas he had only suggested. He thought that we were close and creating together again; I had helped him so much with his work, the greatest of companions for which he was ever indebted to me. I had given him his manhood, but painfully he realized that only now it was blossoming. He now saw me as something "splendid and swift and real and brilliant" and not just an ideal woman. He had brought terrible things upon us, and he prayed that I was not now lost to him forever. He felt as if he was composing his first true love letter, husband to wife, as if all the other letters he had written had been merely adolescent outpourings, and he feared that it was now all too late.

ᔓ   ᔓ   ᔓ

Once his test results were in and the ghost of syphilis laid finally to rest, we spent a week together at my little flat, releasing tensions and being very gentle with one another. We furthered our plans to go to Mexico. Extra luggage, manuscripts, books, etc., we would leave with mother, including the carbon copy of *In Ballast* which Malcolm wanted her to have. Not knowing when we would return, I took most of my clothes. Our intention had been to secure Malcolm's re-entry permit, then spend a short time traveling through Mexico before heading further south.

But as with Villefranche, our plans never worked out as we'd hoped, and this one didn't either.

The last time I saw Ted and Anne together was on September 8, 1936, when they came to see us off on our journey west via Greyhound bus. Peak was there too, and handed me a small copy of *The Bhagavad Gita* with the inscription:

Goodbye, Jan:
And so this is the beginning, not the end:

New life, new hope, new patience, and one day
Your steps will be returning home to find
A friend invisibly with you all the way . . . Peak

We were not to meet again.

೯ ೯ ೯

Visiting mother in 1947, I found that Ted had stopped by and left her
his address. He told me Anne had married someone she'd met while at
the Orpheum and that she seemed content. It was a sad reunion. Teddy
looked much older and had reverted to his Eldon phase: very blond and
quite made up, and obviously scraping by. I had remarried, too, and
our diverging paths had grown unbridgeable. It was our final meeting
after nearly 20 years.

Dustily and endlessly traversing the central plains, I mourned the
soft charm of European countries, their ancient buildings, manageable
landscapes, and quaint towns. It took New Mexico to truly captivate,
especially Santa Fe which I loved, and there we fell in love again. After
ten days in Taos, we could willingly have settled down had not
Malcolm's immigration problem taken precedence.

Taos of course bespoke D. H. Lawrence and Frieda and we made
dutiful pilgrimages. The Taos pueblo recalled Saharan villages save
only for the lack of date palms, and the blankets of the Indians
suggested the burnooses in North African oases. The women,
shawled, impenetrable-eyed, hid their faces from the intrusion of my
camera even as their sisters had at Marrakech. At sunset, Taos pueblo
takes on the reddish hues of the High Atlas adobes, though by day
its structures are subdued.

Navigating Arizona's Painted Desert after dark, we entered
California at dawn. The Colorado River might well have been the
Styx, so silent and unearthly did it seem, and the jagged mountains,
bleak and lifeless, could well have arisen on a prehistoric world, a
lunarscape.

In Hollywood we stayed with John Davenport and his wife Clement, who had a house on El Contento Drive. John was now working on contract for MGM. At Malibu with the Davenports, we visited Edward Weston, the photographer who lived there with Charis Wilson and assorted cats. We marveled at Weston's sensuous studies of bell peppers, many for me evocative of Rodin.

Toward the end of our stay in California we spent a week in San Francisco where we arranged passage to Acapulco on the SS *Pennsylvania* of the Panama Pacific Lines. This was not, as elsewhere reported, a cargo boat, a correction I make merely because the network of fabrications about our marriage has sought to portray us as one step short of bindle stiffs. So, although mutually fond of freighters, this happened not to be one. While in San Francisco we explored Chinatown by night, attended Holy Roller meetings, rode cable cars (of course) and visited Sausalito, where placards tartly proclaimed: THE USE OF THIS PIER FOR ANY PURPOSE WHATSOEVER IS STERNLY FORBIDDEN.

We were good little tourists on our gayest week since leaving Santa Fe.

At 11 P.M., October 25, 1936, we commenced our fateful trip to Mexico. The voyage was prophetically stormy with high tumbling seas. Fortunately I am a good sailor and Malc was in his element. Though our cabin lay smack among the boilers, we were seasoned enough to take that well in stride, and on the morning of November 1, in high and mutual anticipation, we disembarked at Acapulco.

It was All Saints' Day: prelude to the Day of the Dead.

Act Three

. . . the love which us doth,
But Fate so enviously debars,
Is the conjunction of the mind,
And opposition of the stars.

—Andrew Marvell,
"The Definition of Love"

Nineteen thirty-six would be the final year of Acapulco's innocence. As unaffected by the world as a Tunisian village, it was sleepy and primitive, an exotic backwater, filthy, mosquito-ridden, and beautiful.

In place of the voluptuous hotels now crowding its oceanfront, there sprawled a collection of thatched and mud-floored huts spilling forth babies whose brief shifts ended at the genitals. An occasional tethered anteater baked in the noon-hot dust while along the beachfront pelicans swooped and dived, probing for fish. The air was laden with smells of charcoal fires and dung.

We settled at the Miramar, a small hotel close to the beach and plaza. It was clean and modest, dowdy-colonial, frequented by sedate, prolific families. Like the thatched huts and the anteaters it is long gone. Our second-floor room overlooked the street from a small balcony, while its entry, off a common passageway, afforded views of a courtyard with some piglets and the laundry tubs.

On the night following our arrival, it being *Dia de los Muertos,* we visited the cemetery. Families picnicked beside graves decorated with gay flowers. Children clamored for the chocolate skulls and skeletons of *pan de muertos.* We heard soft laughter, an occasional guitar. On this night belonging to the dead, even death itself became cause for celebration.

When we returned to the Miramar, the room felt airless. Cheesecloth, substituting for mosquito netting, served only to enfold the heat. To breathe, we left the door ajar and at dawn, as a faint light crept across the floor, I awoke to perceive a dimly outlined figure beating a stealthy path toward our suitcases.

Without thinking, I sat bolt upright and shouted *Balek!*—a word I'd learned in North Africa to scatter importunate children. It worked equally well in Acapulco, for the man bolted from the room.

Malcolm woke, grumbling sleepily, "Do be quiet. I haven't closed my eyes all night."

When I again stirred, it was to atonal music. Malcolm was dressed and leaning over the balcony studying the street. "A funeral," he explained, looking surprised and happy. "A child's I should think. They have a kind of wonderful jazz band. Come and see." Below, a small cortege unwound . . . an undersized white casket . . . mourners following, and five or six musicians.

We spent the week exploring Acapulco, swimming at Los Hornos and Caleta, and visiting Pie de la Cuesta, then a largely undiscovered spit of land between the ocean and a colorless lagoon. Happily open-minded about germs, we ate and drank everything.

When we left Acapulco it was on Flecha Roja, the Mexico City bus, over a road described in the guidebooks as "unimproved but passable." Our driver spun round the mountain curves, sheer drops, and precipices with total disregard for oncoming vehicles, his motto evidently "plow on regardless."

At Iguala we unclenched our knuckles and decided to cut loose. Though noted for its gold and silver filigree, Iguala to us was notable mainly for its bedbugs. Informed that in Aztec times it had been called Place of the Divinity of the Night, Malcolm remarked sourly that it was obvious no Aztec had stayed at our hotel.

As soon as possible, we moved along to Taxco. The Hotel Melendez, central and reasonable, was mercifully devoid of wildlife. Once again our room would overlook both street and courtyard, with no piglets this time but a fine view of a toilet.

At the house of Doña Berta, who ran a kind of salon, we encountered Alan Mondragon, tall, witty, and a fellow wanderer. With him we visited the studio of Don Valentino, an artist, who apparently also maintained perpetual open house. And there Malcolm fell fatally in love. Introduced to tequila, mescal, and habanera, he embraced all three with such abandon that when it came time to leave, he'd disappeared. Not till next morning was he returned to me, by the *policía,* who'd discover him quite literally sleeping in the gutter and hauled him off to the *cárcel.*

Now limp but grinning, Malcolm remained unabashed, convinced the episode had made "an interesting statement."

A few days later, en route to Mexico City, we re-encountered Alan, and upon arrival, booked rooms at the Hotel Guardiola till we could find a house, for we'd impulsively decided we would share a rental. Calle Humboldt, 62, in Cuernavaca, would have been difficult to resist in any case. Set well back from the street on broad, lush, haphazardly planted grounds, it offered a swimming pool, a pretty tile-roofed house with a 30-foot veranda, three bedrooms, and a breath-taking view of the volcanoes. The monthly tab was forty-two dollars, which we'd split. We moved in November 18.

In varying ways we fell in love with the country, the handsome people, their mocking laughter, and a quality I could only describe as bite. Mornings possessed a special clarity, a brittle freshness, a melange of sounds, cocks, burros, the *carbonero's* cries, and always music, faint but underlying the riot of color so endemic to Mexico.

Our resident gardener was a stocky handsome man named Pedro, who, during the early weeks, was loyalty itself. He waited up for us at night, strung additional wiring along the living room veranda, and called our attention to the pool, clearly in need of paint. Next door we glimpsed a pool of the most extraordinary green and Pedro's suggestion that he color ours met with our full approval.

"Blue," he suggested, and indeed the pool turned out a splendid blue. As we watched it dry, we discussed how large a bonus Pedro should receive. Fortunately we had not yet decided when we checked on it again. In drying in the hot November sun, the paint had sloughed and now lay in dismal strips along the bottom of the pool. Pedro was very much surprised and said it was probably the wrong kind of paint.

We bought another brand, and again he scrubbed the pool and set to work. The paint stayed on in drying and looked most impressive. It took two days and nights to fill the pool, and when the water had risen nearly to the top we went out to admire it. It was a heavenly blue. Closer inspection revealed it really *was* a heavenly blue: all the color was now in the water which, by this time, was positively opaque.

"Oh, hell," Malc said, disgusted. "Just have him clean it out and let it go. It's too bloody hot to be fiddling about this way." Pedro, so informed, said he'd known all along the paint would never do.

Because he spoke Spanish, Alan became our spokesman and arranged with Pedro for a housekeeper. Thus we acquired Josefina, a tidy woman, always stiffly starched, her small face crinkled as a nut. She'd been wife to a soldier in the Mexican Revolution and had borne eleven children (and by as many fathers, Pedro would later claim) though only six survived. It did not occur to us to request references for she was one of Pedro's aunts.

During the early weeks we investigated many nearby towns, especially those holding fiestas, and in December took off for Mexico City for the celebrations at the Shrine of Guadalupe. According to legend, on December 9, 1531, Juan Diego, a poor Indian, had received a visitation from the Virgin seeking a shrine from which to protect "her" *Indios*. When Juan offered his bishop, as proof of the visitation roses plucked from a barren rock to which the Virgin had directed him, her likeness appeared upon the Indian's *tilma* [shirt], and the shrine was born. Of her many fiestas, that of December 12 is the most famous.

There we encountered bedlam.

Pilgrims from every corner of the republic had descended on the square that night. Every possible inch was occupied by worshipers and vendors. Children rode upon their parents' shoulders, babies were slung in rebozos, half-starved dogs slunk between our legs, and fireworks rocketed from the roof of the basilica. We munched tortillas filled with beans and a nameless meat, and poured tequila into our *cervezas*.

Pushed this way, thrust that, often half-suffocated, throngs were elbowing and shoving toward the basilica. One of its tiled domes covers a well whose blackish "holy" water is swallowed hopefully, while relics and curative mud-balls can be bought nearby. The single unifying glue seemed to be poverty. Though the Indian faces revealed varying origins, all were alight with exaltation.

Downing our drinks we found ourselves propelled by worshipers, and in the surging seas lost one another. I caught sight of Alan's tall figure well ahead and thought I could glimpse Malcolm's light brown hair, but the pervasive din drowned out my voice; there was no way to reach them.

How alien we must appear, I thought uneasily, three half-shot gringos defiling their sanctuary, but the sweating, close-packed bodies surged inexorably on, and we were churned into the basilica amid a manic army of the supplicating.

Elbowed on all sides by fanaticism, I felt the swell of claustrophobia, which had bedeviled me since my auto accident. What was I doing here? I, always estranged in mobs? What if I fainted? Would this indomitable juggernaut march blindly over me?

I began gulping air. Only a rising panic enabled me to force an exit through the walls of worshipers. At that, it was after two when I regained the plaza, craving only the familiar sanity of the hotel. Malcolm and Alan did not return till morning.

At Calle Humboldt we added to our staff young Eleodoro who looked ten, claimed to be seventeen, and possessed the beatific smile of a Murillo angel. He ran sundry minor errands and came cheap. We were somewhat startled to learn he smoked pot, drank, and was an indefatigable cocksman.

Considering that Josefina's sister, Trinidad, now did our laundry and made new shirts for Malc, we should have worked as carefree as pampered pets had Malcolm not discovered the cantinas. He would set out with Alan, pencil stubs and notebooks, and then vanish. Alan would phone for reinforcements and we'd spend fruitless hours in pursuit. After some days of this, Alan complained.

"Jan, this is hopeless. He's found so many hidey-holes, I feel like a goddamn duenna. How long does he go on like this?"

"Once he gets started . . ." I said gloomily.

"How did you ever come to marry him?"

I recalled Brock, that New Year's Eve in Paris. He too had asked "Is Malcolm always like this? What in God's name are you marrying him for?"

But Malcolm was not eternally like this. There had been tenderness and productivity and laughter. That was the Malcolm whom I knew and loved. This was the Malcolm with whom I tried to cope. So I ignored the question. We sat on the veranda watching sunset gild the lovely outlines of the two volcanoes, Popocatepetl and his sleeping princess, lovers eternal, eternally star crossed.

"What if we get him out of here?" Alan suggested. "It would have to be someplace small, someplace small and quiet. Fenwick's in Yautepec . . . we might visit him."

"Fenwick? We hardly know him. We've only met him once."

We stared at one another seeking straws to grasp.

"I met him earlier in Taxco. And he *did* ask us to look him up." Frustrated and tired, Alan sounded petulant.

To our relief, Malc accepted the idea and Fenwick, contacted, proved equally amenable. We set out hopefully.

Fenwick had lived in Mexico seven years, mainly in the area of Yautepec, though few were the byways he had not explored. Tall, yellowed, gaunt, with an arc of moustache and a gaze so direct as to seem disconcerting, he made do with a basic simple house: one large room bounded by a screened-in porch, a cubby-hole for his *criada* and her little girl, and a small out-building which served him as an office. He was both writer and photographer.

Candles and lanterns augmented electricity, although an improvised shower and the privy were outdoors. Primitive amenities or not, Fenwick had made his habitation colorful and appealing. Our visit, however, did not work out as we'd hoped. We spent a single night, roused far too early by a reveille of sunlight.

"Tell you what," Malcolm proposed with one of his charming smiles, "Let's get out of here and go to Cuautla. I've had more than enough of pissing into the wind, and there's not a bloody thing worth doing here."

In Cuautla we'd met a film maker from the capital and together had visited not only the mineral baths but a river of cantinas. It was not a reassuring memory. And true to form, while we were checking in at the Hotel San Diego, Malc made his getaway, insisting that he needed cigarettes. He'd eaten nothing since the night before.

Although we hastened to give chase, Malc managed cannily to stay one cantina ahead, and after an hour Alan called a halt. "Jan, listen to me please. Malc could be leading us around like this for days. Do you have any Veronal?"

I shook my head. I'd never taken a sleeping pill nor, so far, needed one.

"Well," he said firmly, "we've got to get some now. If we don't knock him out we could lose him altogether and then Lord knows what could happen to him. I *knew* we should have stayed in Yautepec. At least it's small."

At a pharmacy, we had no trouble buying Veronal. Our problem was locating Malc. When we caught up with him, he was embellishing his favorite fantasy: he'd flown for the Loyalists in Spain and been shot down over Toledo, or Valladolid, or San Sebastian, or Avila. At this very moment Franco was sending operatives to flush him out.

Generally docile about medication, Malcolm swallowed the Veronal with a slug of mescal. It had absolutely no effect.

"We'll wait a bit," Alan decided, disappointedly, "then try another one." The suggestion left me apprehensive. In *Big Blonde,* Dorothy Parker's lady attempted suicide with a similar concoction. I could see the headlines: AMERICAN WOMAN AND PARAMOUR MURDER ENGLISH WRITER. In any threesome, no matter how oddly assembled (for Alan was gay), the third leg of the triangle is forever "paramour." CLAIM OVERDOSE ACCIDENTAL, it would jocularly conclude.

After a second Veronal, we watched Malc nervously. By mid-afternoon he was sleepy enough for us to coax him back to the hotel. Once in the room, however, he became rambunctious and, announcing that his bed would cripple him, demanded we place its mattress on the floor. By now at our wits' ends, we humored him.

At this point I needed a solitary walk, so Alan went off alone to the mineral baths. I passed a cinema featuring Maria Felix and Pedro Armendariz, sat for a time in the plaza with my eyes closed, making my mind a blank, ate *huachinango* at a nearby restaurant, and eventually returned to the hotel.

When I entered our room, the mattress was on the floor but Malc had vanished. Too weary to contemplate pursuit, I flung myself down upon it and fell asleep.

Malcolm did not return, but when I awoke my mind was astonishingly clear.

I found Alan in the restaurant where he was having breakfast. "Where's Malc?" he greeted me.

"I wish I knew. When I got back to the room last night, he was already gone."

"My God, Jan, the damned bus leaves in half an hour! Oh, I can't stand this, not again! I've missed more damn fiestas chasing Malc!" He set his cup down sharply. Coffee slopped. "Well, come on, then, don't just stand there! Let's go back to the plaza and start all over."

But I sat down alongside. "Look, Alan," I began, my voice wavering somewhat, "I hate to say this but perhaps if Malc and I were by ourselves . . . he really can't drink, you know, and when you do, it starts him off with four drinks to your one. Perhaps if we were alone again, he just might be all right." (At least until another Alan swam into our lives.)

"Well!" said Alan. "Well, really. This isn't very nice of you, Jan."

Petulant, tired, hung over, he fished in his trousers where the pockets bulged over his large soft hips, and pulled out his cigarettes. From force of habit he handed me one and lit it. His prominent blue eyes stared, accusingly, wounded, one more rejection in a life of many. I knew he might miss the rambling adobe house we'd found together, the pool, the jungled garden, but not Malcolm and not me. For a brief moment, ours had been his axis; now he would rattle off, and rattle on, momentarily untethered.

"Oh, Alan," I said, "I shall miss you. But I can't help myself."

He shrugged. "Come on," he said. "Let's try unearthing him again. If we can get another Veronal into him we just might get him home . . . though what good that will do . . . The hell with the bus. When we find him, we'd better take a cab. And keep the Veronal hidden when I go. Don't let him get his mitts on it." It was typical of him to hang in there till the last: a lesser man might have said, "To hell with you then, toots. Go hunt for him yourself."

But it had been the right decision. Through the ensuing months, with minor deviations, Malcolm and I achieved a productive happiness we'd not known since our good months in New York. He worked on his newly conceived *Under the Volcano,* and as always, I typed his finished notes and worked, too, on my dance-hall story—for with Alan gone, what had been eliminated was the merciless duration of Malcolm's binges.

But lacking Alan, I now had to deal with Pedro; my Spanish might be miserable, but Malc's was nonexistent. Our paragon was suddenly a mule of a less-appealing hue. He treated the garden as his enemy, vanished for hours at a stretch, sold our pretty roses in the marketplace, ignored all references to the pool which was turning green, and did nothing that I asked.

Revisiting the capital to obtain extensions of our permits, we were confronted on our return with a fearless-looking girl whom Pedro introduced as Marguerita. She assessed us carefully, toured the grounds, inspected Pedro's room, and deigned to stay. In no time at all, Josefina's feathers were as permanently ruffled as a hen's, and it was obvious arrangements were not going well. Compelled at last to bring matters to a head, I encountered the full force of his belligerence.

He could not work, he announced defiantly, because he was ill and needed to be nursed by Marguerita. He could not work because to be in the same house as his aunt, a *sinvergüenza,* a scoundrel, whom, God forgive him, he had recommended, had rendered him *enfermo.* He could not work because the means for irrigation were inadequate: no pipes, no usable hoses, and no peons. Bernardino, one of his uncles and the next-door gardener, had 5 peons no less. But Pedro could not work because he lacked fit tools and would not work because it was Señora Baldwin, the villa's owner, who had hired him and who paid his wages and whose orders, *solamente,* he would take.

Warming to his subject, he announced that had I been a man he would have knocked me down, and he climaxed his performance by giving immediate notice. To my pleas that he at least finish out the week, he turned a stone-deaf ear.

Two days later we were served with papers by the *Conciliacion,* threatening that unless we at once rehired our gardener, so wrongfully discharged, we must, by law, compensate him to the extent of three months' wages, totaling 159 pesos.

Luckily, three factors favored us: Pedro's insistence that he was hired and paid by the Señora Baldwin, thus shifting the responsibility to her; the eager testimony of Josefina, finally ensconced in her long-coveted room; and the abilities of the Señora's friend and *abogado,* Don Tomas. Still, it alerted us, and I notified the Señora that henceforth we'd pay the gardener ourselves.

Don Pablo was the choice of Josefina. He had been living with her mother, her sister and brother-in-law, her six surviving children and two nephews, three pigs, a flock of chickens, and a horse, and he was understandably eager to find work. The chickens had been especially *grosseros.*

He was thin as a reed and very tall, and his sallow face was both weak and charming. Asked about gardening, he replied he'd been a government *obrero,* a soldier, and barkeep in a *pulqueria.* It didn't sound too functional but we had no other candidates. He was accompanied by Juana, a full-lipped girl with many bouncing parts.

Don Pablo was an essentially simple soul, and we shortly learned to evaluate his strengths and weaknesses, Juana, and a fondness for *pulque.* He was willing and deferential but allergic to energy, and he had a profound disregard for the elements of horticulture.

The seeds we bought him usually did not come up at all, but when they did, they rose dramatically in the wrong places. Lettuce sprouted among petunia and dahlia beds; carrots and onions bordered our front paths; and when I bought grass seed for the ground behind the pool, Don Pablo convinced us both that it would never take, and developed his own system for transplanting grass, blade by blade, from another area. Four weeks of this produced only furtive vegetation and we prevailed upon him, for he was fond of squatting, to abandon the project and just let nature be.

On Alan's departure, I had appropriated his room. Like Malc's, it opened onto the veranda. Malcolm had long complained about his bedstead, iron with innumerable protuberances. He needed a worktable and we both needed bookcases. Highly recommended by the inestimable Josefina, we contacted one Don Antonio, reputedly a carpenter, who arrived blithe, carefree, open-browed, and totally devoid of tools. Unable to take measurements, he fell back on elegant sketches tending largely to the baroque.

"How about *some* straight lines?" Malc demanded. "I don't want *everything* circular."

The next day Antonio bought his tape and took careful measurements. He figured intensely, then announced "25 pesos."

I knew the routine well. "Twenty," I said.

He knew the routine too. "Twenty-one pesos," he countered.

"Done," I conceded, and we both looked pleased.

Next he requested money for the materials and we started over. "How much?" I asked.

"Ten pesos." He regarded me soulfully from his liquid eyes and I had a mental lapse. I must have, for I handed over 10 pesos to him with no mention of a receipt, inquiring only "When can we have the lot?" It was then Sunday.

He studied me and said "Saturday?"

"Thursday," I said from force of habit but he topped me. "For you, dear lady, I will bring tomorrow the bed parts. The rest next day. Or Thursday." We were mutually enchanted.

Enchantment lasted for four days after which I dispatched the slightly less inestimable Josefina to find out what the hell had happened to him. "He says *mañana, Señora.*"

⤶ ⤶ ⤶

Belatedly, light dawned. I advised Don Antonio I had bought *sabroso pulque* just for him. Caramba and behold! The bookcases and the table arrived within the week and were followed by the long-awaited bedstead. Very nice they were too. *Mordida* [bribery] takes many forms, but in Mexico, as in Paris, it was mother's milk. I'd been a little slow in learning it.

To Josefina we gave the red iron bed and let her select a mattress to complete it. She was enormously proud; it appeared she'd never owned either.

In mid-January we acquired two stray pussycats whom I longed to name Oedipuss and Priapuss but who became, in deference to Mexico, Chicharro and Xicottencatl. They were talented felines. Our veranda floor was composed of large black and white square tiles in a checkerboard pattern and onto these the cats would fit themselves as adeptly as a pair of models. When it came to pets, Malcolm and I were ardent ailurophiles.

But there were darker days. On January 14 I wrote of one:

> I am really fed up with this place today. The rats eat my clothes in
> the cupboard. This morning I found that the lovely little sweater I
> got in Vienna had an enormous hole chewed out of its back, and my
> sweet velvet hat has lost half its feathers . . . The maid's sister parks
> her horse to graze in our front garden, under our very eyes . . . There
> is always the charming expectation that a scorpion will drop through
> the roof tiles onto one's head, and always Malcolm's favorite diver-
> sion: quarreling over a meal. I am down once more with nervous
> indigestion and in a raging temper.
>
> And yet everything had started rippingly, we were to go to
> Tepoztlan this afternoon, plans were all made, Josefina had pro-
> duced a delicious lunch, so Malc, as usual, had to dig up something
> we could quarrel about. (In the future I shall insist on eating in my
> room . . . this endless spattering and jabbing over coffee has gone too
> long: it unfits me for anything more useful than hysteria . . .)

But like most of our spats now, this one proved to be short-lived. That night Malcolm tucked the following note under my door:

I do love you so please forgive me
Soon we will take a little trip to Jojutla
or to the grutas or perhaps to Cuautla
you looked very beautiful tonight don't leave me please sleep well
tonight my dearest
and tomorrow we will retrieve we.

When Malc wanted to be charming, it was impossible for me to resist him. Needless to say, I did not take my meals alone.

Insects were an ongoing problem. A large pea-green and very fuzzy caterpillar fell into Malc's shorts while he was shaving and bit him. Mindful of Fenwick's warnings, I rushed him to a doctor who gave him a prescriptive salve for the welt which formed. It was commonplace to see ants dragging a huge tarantula up an outside wall. And once, when I stepped on a fat spider, it broke open (like a piñiata), scattering hundreds of minute baby spiders in all directions. I got stung by bees (Josefina applied mud), and there was a memorable encounter with umbrella ants. Rats, of course, and praying mantises we had aplenty; also something large and clumsy which clung to the roof tiles at night and coughed. But somehow I never saw a snake.

Calle Humboldt awakened surprising nesting instincts. I painted all the doors, made spreads and curtains, and even created lampshades out of wire which I covered with the curtain fabric. I was quite pleased with my maiden results though my technique was, charitably, questionable. Paint today can be used as it comes from the can but enamel, in 1937, required much thinning. Blissfully unaware of this, I slathered on a gluey substance which fought every stroke of the brush.

Malc's bedroom doors remained red; those to the connecting bedroom, blue; but for my bedroom I reserved my favorite color, black. With black, white, and gray serapes covering the twin cots, and "monk's-cloth" drapes and lampshades, the room achieved what might today be called a minimalist quality. I should add that in the thirties, monk's cloth was the fabric of choice for studio decor: it worked easily and it came cheap.

When I eventually put away my thimble, it was to get back to work. I had decided that *The Dead Ride Hard* (my working title for the miners of Pécs) should by rights be a trilogy rather than a single novel—the first period encompassing the Hungarian revolution and subsequent White Terror, then the hero Antal, life in America, and finally the story of the mines and strikes. It was a hopelessly ambitious project with research facilities in Cuernavaca slim to nonexistent. Reluctantly I laid aside my copious notes to concentrate on the dance-hall book with its more modest cast of hundreds.

We took long daily walks, tossing discussions of our projects back and forth, singing our improvised doggerel, aware of deepening ties. And presently we added a fresh activity.

From the Casino de la Selva on the outskirts of the town, we rented horses. I had never been on a horse and was doubly skittish since in Taxco we'd encountered a young couple, the Beims, and learned that Lorraine Beim's limp resulted from a riding accident in Central Park. We set out, therefore, at a sober pace, and before long were riding two and three days a week, visiting nearby villages. I maintained twin caveats: that my mount be elderly and sedate, and that I would on no account argue with him. All the sheep-dip about letting your horse know who is master seemed the height of idiocy: my horse *knew* already who was master—it had only to look at me. So if it wanted to dog the footsteps of Malcolm's steed, that was fine with me; but if it longed for its stables and its feedbag and its family, that was as Allah willed.

Never to experience that passionate sense of freedom born of galloping recklessly across moor and fen (à la *Wuthering Heights*), as an athlete I would remain tentative. Only once did I gallop. My horse, startled by a small dog, broke free, and I unexpectedly found the gallop far easier to enjoy than the trots and canters with which I'd experimented. When I wrote mother of our rides, to my surprise she approved: "So good for the liver," she wrote. But bouncing about and clutching the pommel with both hands, I was never a dashing figure, and as an equestrienne I was dubbed by Malcolm the damsel in distress, which I thought tolerant of him.

On one occasion we extended our wanderings to Tepoztlán, a small village with some interesting relics of the ancient civilizations, intending to scale the pyramids. Here Malc easily outclimbed me. A somewhat portly gazelle, he mounted to the *tepozteco* at the tip of the pyramid, while I at the halfway mark collapsed breathless on the ancient stones.

We also visited Chapultepec Springs and the lively waterfall at Salto de San Anton. It was on one such trip—to Cuautla in this case— that the episode recounted in *Under the Volcano* occurred: that of the dying Indian found lying in the road. Malcolm and I and Alan were on the bus together and I remember that we got out to see what was happening. Many of the other passengers got out, too, fascinated by death and dying. Anyway, we were warned, as gringos, not to get involved. So none of us intervened, but later, when the bus moved on, we discovered that a passenger, a *pelado* (penniless drunk), had stolen money from the dying man and was proudly exhibiting it. But nobody could or would do anything about it. What was there that one could do?

Malc has depicted this as taking place in "Tomalin," though I do not know of such a village in that vicinity. There is, however, a Tomellin en route from Tehuacan to Oaxaca, with a ravine and a river of the same name, and wildly lovely scenery. It may be that during his later and fateful weeks in Oaxaca, he came to know of this and that the music of the name appealed to him.

In February we again spent a few days with Fenwick and, on this occasion at least, the two men appeared compatible, discovering mutual interests in psychic research and the tarot. Malcolm was on his best behavior and our candlelight dinners seemed infinitely romantic.

March broke hot and dry. The rains were not due for several months and the garden showed their lack. We took to lingering over breakfasts, even lunch would come and go as we remained absorbed in our discussions—there was always so much to say. With no one else have I enjoyed this total communication.

That month, too, our petition to enter Mexico as *rentistas* was granted thanks to Señora Baldwin's *abogado* who stood bond for us . . . an act I'm afraid he must subsequently have regretted deeply.

"to enter Mexico as rentistas"

With our *rentista* status clarified, we planned to visit Oaxaca, but this was frustrated when one morning I found Malcolm bent double, unable to straighten up. Sciatica was diagnosed, and Malcolm put to bed. By the thirteenth, finally improved, he announced firmly that he had grown stir-crazy and wanted to see a film. I had been making a bedspread and curtain for his room which were so nearly ready that I was bent on finishing them.

"You don't mind then if I go?"

"Of course not. It'll do you good. When you return, you can admire my handiwork."

As he was leaving, he paused, turned, and smiled at me.

"Well if you're sure," he said doubtfully." Anyway, I should be home about eleven."

"Good, I'll wait up and we can have some coffee."

"No, don't do that," he said. "You look a little tired. Watch you don't strain your eyes."

He rolled through the room with his sailor's gait, and through the dining room and out into the darkness. I caught a glimpse of him as he passed under the great jacaranda tree and from its circle of light into the thick Mexican evening.

Josefina had left after supper to spend the night with her sister, and the stillness, magnified by Malcolm's diminishing footsteps, moved like a living presence within our low white house. Its isolation engulfed me.

Springing to my feet, I caught up a sweater and ran out onto the path calling, "Malc, wait for me, Malc!"

Where our drive met Calle Humboldt, I stopped. The unlit, unpaved street, punctuated only by faint squares of lantern light spilling from dirt-floored rooms, presented endless blackness and a silence broken now by the nearby snarling of two dogs in combat. I called Malc once again, more loudly this time.

Hoof beats rang out as a horse galloped past; for a brief instant I glimpsed the shadowy outline of its rider. The man's voice hallooed in drunkenness, and I ran back toward the shelter of the house.

The tropics seemed to magnify the night, giving it a texture and a depth like pile. I was swallowed up in it. The clock read seven-thirty.

Two hours for the movie, perhaps more. An hour there and back.
Malcolm had said he would be home about eleven. I resumed work on
his bedspread, its stripes as boldly colored as a baby's blocks.

By eleven I'd set aside the spread to hang Malc's curtain. I turned
down his bed, yawned, and thought about a bath. There was no gas;
our water heater burned only kindling. When lit, it rumbled fiercely. I
distrusted it. To hear my own voice, I spoke aloud. "Tomorrow, then,
I'll shower in the morning."

Where *was* Malc? The clock read eleven-twenty.

From the kitchen, I brought the long-handled feather duster.
Holding it upside down, I moved through the bedrooms and bath,
carefully knocking the small brown scorpions from the walls and
ceilings and stamping on them with my thick huaraches. At night, they
eased through the roof tiles and through the beams and rafters, and once
I'd found one on my pillow when I waked. I killed the last visible
scorpion and put away the duster . . . 11:35 .

Could Malc have met somebody? But whom? Outside of Mexico
City, we knew no one.

Once more I picked up the spread and tried to concentrate, but I
was taking long uneven stitches and glancing often at the door. A bar?
He hadn't been in one without me for three months, nearly four, not
since I'd suggested to Alan that he move on . . . ("for every glass you
hoist, Malcolm hoists four . . .")

I struggled with the shadowy fears of memory and imagination . . .
the night two drunken Mexicans had galloped past us on the road,
bawling "Silverio Perez," and brandishing machetes. One had made an
only partly playful run at us, and Malc later insisted it hadn't been all
that playful. It had been just about this time of night. I rose abruptly,
seeing Malcolm lying on the road, hearing, as I'd heard earlier that
evening, the retreating gallop of a horse and the long drunken bellow-
ings. "Nonsense!" I said, my voice meant to somehow reassure. "Mor-
bid and silly. I mustn't think such things."

But I could no longer concentrate upon the spread. I circled the
room, picked up a book, and for the next hour vainly tried to read. At

1:15 I tossed the book aside and stepped onto the veranda. The moon had risen and the outlines of the imperturbable volcanoes shadowed the horizon. I sat on the adobe railing and stared toward them.

"Where *is* Malcolm? What has happened to him? He has almost no money." Yet Malcolm was a foreigner, a gringo, and to *descamisados* all gringos were surely millionaires. I paced the length of the veranda, growing chilled, aware I was becoming incoherent.

An unseen animal leaped noisily to the roof tiles, clattered across them, and sprang with a thud and a smashing of boughs into the thicket below. I rubbed my palms along my thighs, breathed deeply. From the thicket rose a series of sharp coughs. Possum? Coon? Wildcat? Or? I ran back into the house and slammed the door.

"Malcolm," I whispered, breathing his name as though in prayer. The intimation of loss was choking me. "He had to meet someone; he *had* to. But then where is he? What has happened to him?"

Coffee might help. I moved toward the kitchen. But the charcoal bed on which Josefina cooked had died. I stared stupidly at the twin baskets of kindling and charcoal. (Oh God what a country!) The great iron and tile stove squatted, massive, impervious, and useless on its cement floor, studded with the *cazuelas* and the *ollas* I had thought more picturesque than mere pots and pans. *It had been my idea, this year in Mexico.*

The recognition left its load of guilt. I had a paralyzing vision of arranging Malcolm's funeral as panic banished all but the endearing memories. A man above all men whose like I would not find again. "Oh please let him be safe!"

 The police? But in this land the *policía* were a last resort. Bedeviled by bewilderment and fear, I drifted back to Malcolm's room and lay across his bed.

And then at dawn I heard a blessed clatter: Josefina! As I burst into the kitchen she whirled, startled. *"Senora! Esta usted enferma?"* Sick? *"Pero yo no, Jose, pero el señor."* And in my kitchen Spanish I explained. A wise sly look possessed her nutlike face. *"Aie, Señora,"* she said, making a tippling gesture. I shook my head. How could I make her understand?

"Pablo? Don Pablo? When does he arrive?"

"*Pues. Señora,* he is already here."

Together we ran along the path to where Don Pablo squatted musingly among the roses. "Search all the bars, all the cantinas," Josefina bade him.

"The hospital," I urged.

And as he took off at a loping gait, Josefina stood on tiptoe, shrieking after him, "The jail, you understand, *el carcel . . . el carcel!*"

I returned to the house to pour out on the typewriter all the pain and the terror I was feeling: "Nothing in life means anything to me beside my husband. He is heart's blood, the breath of life itself, the work I hope to do, the peace I long to have, kindness and goodness, gentleness and generosity far above all men. The years I have passed with him are such as one might dream of . . . for sweetness and happiness and closeness they've been everything I might envision love to be. I could not live without Malcolm. Some part of me might breathe and function but life would become barren. God, what is this I am writing? Malcolm and I are one! What befalls either of us befalls both of us!"

Here I broke off.

Silently, Josefina and I drank coffee in the kitchen. Then came a shuffling sound out in the drive and in the morning light Malcolm emerged, staggering boldly.

For a moment, as I dashed toward him, I pursued my fantasies of violence. A victim? Stabbed? My glance probed him like a surgeon's, disheveled, yes, and stained. Bedraggled even, but obviously whole. No blood, no sling or tourniquets, his face unpummeled and his clothes untorn, but from him arose, like a roll of drums, the triumphant fumes of alcohol. I felt, rather than saw, Josefina slip from my side to move back to the house.

"Buenas dias," Malcolm said, bowing elaborately. "Jan, my little, little, little Jan, Jan, you are very *guapa* [pretty]."

And then the night, long as a polar season, broke, and I heard my voice, prayerful till now, in its pain and terror, numbness and agony, transmuted at the sight of him, raging like lava against this profanation.

∽ ∽ ∽

Holy week began March 22. The entire length of Calle Guerrero was roped off and *pulquerias* were installed to form a central lane. It abounded with Ferris wheels, pole dancers, tent shows and fireworks, and the inevitable vendors. Both Jardin Morelos and Jardin Juarez became one vast fairground. By day and night they throbbed to the beat of regional dances. Within the tents, vaudeville acts convulsed their audiences. Outside, replicas of Judas, straw-stuffed, were set afire and rocketed aloft at imminent peril to the onlookers as strands of flaming straw erupted groundward. The *Indios,* childlike in their enthusiasms, watched everything with delight. The mestizos watched more cannily.

Unfortunately, the bacchanalian aspects of these revels proved too much for Malcolm, as I noted in writing Alan:

Got your card this morning. How I envy you, returning to the States. We have put so much of time, money and ourselves into this place that it is rather like being enamored of an octopus. However, it is looking lovely.

Our Malcolm has been "whimsical" since yesterday evening. He arrived home at 2 A.M. and departed as abruptly as though shot from a gun at 9. "A walk," he explained quaintly. Some kind soul we ran into at the Cadillac Bar last night, an Englishman living in Canada, phoned to tell me he had "seen" him. I should damned well think so! It's almost the first real break for months, and I suppose might be attributed to overwork.

Our wilderness makes me feel like St. Francis without his birds, and at night, the solitude is devastating. Do I miss your company and your sense of humor? Guess!

Malc gave me a long talk this morning about his "baser" nature. It would of course be right that he should stay here and send Pablo to bring beer, but his "baser" nature had him in its grip and his "baser" nature told him he must walk. So walk he would. And did.

Several nights later, when we'd turned in early, for once, we were waked by a hearty rendering of "*Las Mananitas.*" Our troubadours emerged as Ed and Mary Feeney, whom we met through Alan. In Cuernavaca to observe the fiesta, they had found the hotels full.

We fixed up cots and sat talking until well past three. The Feeneys were New Yorkers, intelligent and politically active. I admired Mary's dedication, and for some time I had been faced uncomfortably with my own lack of commitment. Vocally honest, yes, but always that judgmental core, questioning, analyzing, ultimately inert.

Ed was an artist. Though Mary made me feel frivolous, I could talk to Ed. She was straight on; Ed was another story. "I wish I could live my life the way you two are doing," he told me wistfully. Probably he would have liked to be Gauguin, erupting from the limitations of his neat existence to pursue a star, even to the terrible beauty of a small Pacific Island. And yet he never would.

Malc was his opposite. Lacking that deadly talent for the ordinary, he wrote through every sober and most drunken moments, writing as from his pores, until his prose flowed rich as ancient brandy. Terrors and insecurities would not release him: "*My God! What shall I do without my misery?*"

When the Feeneys left, we escaped to Mexico City for a week, making the Hotel Canada there our headquarters. Convenient and inexpensive, it enabled us to sample a variety of modest indulgences, for once again Malcolm's allowance positioned us in Fat City.

And by now we had friends in Mexico City; Marcia and Alfred Miller, who worked for the Cardenas regime, and Ethel and Manolo Cervantes, who made us aware of the dangers posed by the Sinarquistas and Christeros and their clerico-fascist movement known as El Christo Rey. Terrorists, these groups conducted raids, massacring or mutilating professors in nonclerical schools, and waging unceasing warfare against public school instructors. They were especially virulent in San Luis Potosi where they cut off the hands of teachers who defied their fanaticism. In his book *Falange,* published in 1943, Allan Chase gives an excellent overview of this powerful instrument, trained by Nazi

agents throughout Latin America along Gestapo lines and forged in
Mexico under the aegis of General Wilhelm Von Faupel as part of the
vast network of Falange espionage, propaganda, smuggling, murder,
and torture.

When we returned to Cuernavaca, we immersed ourselves in work.
We wrote, we talked, we laughed a great deal, and Malc drank only
moderately. There seemed good cause for optimism. Then occurred a
situation so bizarre as to activate Malcolm's predilection for the inexplicable. The following year, in a letter to his father seeking help for
Malc, I referred to this in detail:

> . . . as you know, Malcolm was working hard on two novels, nearly
> completed: *In Ballast to the White Sea* and *Under the Volcano*. In the
> former, the hero is an undergraduate who, voyaging to Norway, even
> as Malcolm did, encountered his doppelganger, a novelist Malcolm
> has named William Erikson.
>
> In the latter, the leading figure is a former British consul living
> in Mexico [this profession no doubt suggested by the fact that an
> American vice-consul lived next door]. In Malcolm's book, he is a
> brilliant drunkard, murdered in one of his drunken peregrinations,
> whose body is then tossed into the chasmlike gorge which bisects the
> town. Both characters were, of course, versions of Malc himself.
>
> On the day after he completed the aforementioned scene, we
> strolled to the plaza, where almost immediately, in that day's head-
> lines, we read that an American tourist had been murdered at Taxco.
> We bought the paper and discovered that the man had arrived only
> the previous evening from the States, that little or nothing was known
> of him, that he had been drinking heavily, had apparently been
> robbed before he was slain by his attackers. His body was tossed into
> the gorge. His name was William Erikson!
>
> To many, this would have appeared at worst an unnerving
> coincidence. To Malcolm it became a portent and a judgment. He
> felt he had somehow murdered the hapless tourist since it was he
> who had created not only the man but the conditions of his death

. . . which may well have been intended for him—Malcolm—until the intervention of his character. No matter that Erikson appeared in one novel and the death scene in another: that only infused both of them with disaster. Although these connotations seemed, with time, to pass, Malcolm remained excited and conjunctionally badly shaken.

～ ～ ～

By April the heat had become blinding. The garden suffered and we curtailed our walks. And presently we underwent invasion: an army of umbrella ants, over half an inch long, many of them winged, spilling across our landscape, uncountable and endless. In minutes they razored the hibiscus and oleanders and littered the ground with a confetti of torn blossoms. The squirming bodies consumed every visible leaf on plant and shrub and towards noon attacked the adobe wall of our veranda. Within hours they were swarming inside it by the thousands.

I had never beheld such utter voraciousness or such absorbed destruction. They were as efficient as machines of war. We poured kerosene by the gallon over them, Flit, creosote, even boiling water, but for each destroyed two came to take its place. Finally Bernardino, the next-door gardener, rescued us: for 15 pesos he rented us his Cyanogas pump and thus, at long last, the destruction of the nests began.

Poor Pablo worked among the ants, shaking himself like a dog with fleas as they crawled on his feet or rampaged up his legs. It took days to clear them totally and then repair the damage they had caused. The hole in the veranda wall alone was as large as a dinner plate.

Between the fate of William Erikson and the plague of ants, it was time for our long-delayed visit to Oaxaca. On Wednesday, April 21, we set out from the capital via narrow-gauge railway by night, in a third-class carriage with sharp wooden benches.

I had often traveled third class in Europe and North Africa, but this was truly spartan. By turns, we dozed upon each other's shoulders.

Having left Mexico City at 5 P.M. on the twenty-first, when we arrived in Oaxaca well after 8 next morning, even our teeth felt gritty.

Oaxaca lies beneath the jagged peaks of the Sierras, its soil as rosy as that of Marrakech. Spanish architecture lends dignity and serenity . . . a town for languor and the pursuit of dreams. From the Cerro del Fortin spread a gardened vista of pastel houses studded with barred windows and balconies and carved wooden doors, a déjà vu of the Spain where we had met. We discovered arcades, pillared as those in Italy, and paused at outdoor cafes where patrons lingered over dominoes.

That afternoon, a dirt road took us to Monte Alban where, rising from a hill a thousand feet above the valley of Oaxaca, the Zapotecs had built their City of the Gods. Its temples and its tombs once covered miles and were still undergoing restoration. For a long time we sat on the broad stairway, so vast in its conception and its execution, and marveled at the ancient architects who had wrought such miracles of stone.

Another dirt road led us next day to Mitla with a stop en route at the 2000-year-old cypress of Santa Maria del Tule, once worshipped by the Indians as a god of growth. Hugely wide, 160 feet in height, it was quite possibly the oldest living thing, and for Malcolm, admittedly something of a tree freak, this living relic held a sacred quality.

At the village of Mitla, sun-baked and picturesque, wild fig trees grew in the plazas while organ cacti bordered the narrow streets. Long before the advent of Cortez, Mitla was known as Mictlan, City of the Dead. It bore great religious significance in the flourishing civilization of that time. The workmanship of its temples and tombs and walls is stunning, and the geometric patterns woven so skillfully in stone were copied in much of the local embroidery we saw. More sophisticated than the ruins of Monte Alban, its Hall of Monoliths boasted eight enormous columns, each wrought from an individual stone block.

Our guide became, too, something of a friend, acquainting us with the less *conocido* parts of town, including a *casa de las delicias*. The ladies there, though disapproving of my presence, were obviously intrigued by Malcolm. Compared to the *maisons de joie* I'd visited in Paris and North Africa, this sad little brothel revealed an odd blend of innocence and savagery.

In all we spent four crowded memorable days and determined to repeat the visit at more length before leaving Mexico. (It was a commitment only Malc would undertake, and then, disastrously.) Though we had planned to stop in Mexico City to round out our week, Malcolm's sciatica acted up on the return trip, which headed us instead, and hastily, for home.

By the middle of May, though he still occasionally used a walking stick, Malcolm was decidedly improved. The cats played their games on the checkerboard of the veranda. The rains came, driving off dust and lassitude. And Mephistopheles appeared full blown in our midst, sprung not from flame and brimstone but in the rotund persona of Malcolm's father-surrogate, that bottle-a-day bard with full blown sexual neuroses: Conrad Aiken.

On May the twenty-first, a Friday, the awkward wall phone, hung just too high for comfort, jangled while Malcolm and I were at lunch. Josefina, padding from the kitchen with the inevitable stuffed peppers, grabbed at it. *"Bueno? Es para usted, Senor,"* she cried, leaving the receiver dangling and plopping the *cazuela* between us.

Malc, looking vaguely threatened as he always did with representations of authority, fingered the receiver. "Yes? Who? Yes. *Who?* Great balls of fire!" He broke off in midshout, and half speaking into the phone, half turned to me, he cried: *"It's Conrad!* Of course come down. *He's in Mexico City!* But you'll stay with us of course! Look, there's a bus, Estrella de Oro, it leaves from the Zocalo, the plaza, around noon. We'll meet you when you get in."

He talked a few more moments, then returned to the table. "Crazy bastard. Jerry wouldn't give him a divorce. That's why he's here, to get one. Mary's along, and Ed, Ed Burra. They'll stay with us of course."

Still talking, he began to eat. "It'll take a month after he locates a lawyer. Jerry mustn't know about Mary. She'd queer things somehow. They'll get married as soon as the divorce comes through."

"Poor Jerry," I said, recalling that without Jerry's intervention, I'd never had met Malcolm. "Remember that time you brought home a copy of *Ideal Marriage* and Conrad cried, 'For God's sake don't let Jerry see it!' What's Mary like? Who is she?"

Malc looked past me, considering. "An artist, I think. Docile, most probably. Conrad says with delight that she is inarticulate."

"Was Jerry too articulate?" I tried to keep my voice carefully neutral.

"Jerry," said Malcolm, "was a bitch."

"Then an unsatisfied bitch. Anyhow, I liked her. I liked her quite a lot. Conrad can't have been much of a romp with all those complexes."

As Josefina slip-slopped back into the dining room with some quivering dessert, Malcolm shrugged. "Well, when you're a child and catch your father strangling your mother . . ."

"Strangling? It wasn't strangling last time you told the story. You told me that he shot her."

"Well, wot the hell," said Malcolm. "She stayed just as dead; matter of fact, they both did, and anyhow the other version seems more colorful."

I was trying to recall all he had told me about Conrad Aiken. "Perhaps it's his New England heritage . . . all that *sturm und drang* behind those immaculate and snowy walls," Malc said. But such tales as I remembered frightened me for our tranquillity as yet so new and fragile.

"I'll move into the blue bedroom. Conrad and Mary can have mine. Yours and mine are the only ones that have two beds."

"Oh he'll *like* that," Malcolm said. "Where will we put Ed Burra? Remember him? From Spain?"

"Good God, where will we put him? He'll have to sleep on the veranda on that *awful* couch. The mattress is cornhusks, or newspapers, or anyhow something noisy."

"Well, he's alone," Malcolm grinned impishly. "The noise won't bother anyone."

Conrad Aiken did not wear a beard or a cloak or a large hat or colorful vests: he looked, in fact, at first sight, like a Midwestern banker, or an accountant, or an alderman—large, florid, balding. Yet he could transform two companions into a retinue, and his cold, arrogant, light-blue gaze above the ruddiness of his flesh displayed the decisive shrewdness of the Recording Angel. And I recalled Malcolm relating with malicious glee how, in the anthologies of verse Conrad had edited, he'd reserved the major coverage always for himself.

He now descended from the bus on heavy feet and turned to help a large girl with a withdrawn expression, and a tiny kernel of a man, like a shrunken bantam weight, who was carrying a duffel bag. In the tropical extravagance of the Mexican plaza, they resembled a seedy troupe forever touring the provinces. Greetings were fumbling and without warmth, except between Aiken and Malc who clasped each other, father and son, prelate and acolyte.

With Mary and Ed Burra, I helped the driver extricate their luggage. When we rejoined the two writers, their reconciliation was complete: their shared experiences of Cambridge, England, and of Cambridge, Mass., had erased the intervening years. Each of them florid, large in frame, sea-blue of eye; they greeted their luggage-bearers. "We're going to Charlie's Place to have a drink!"

Did I only imagine a church bell tolling as I followed them? In any case, the pattern of our days was set.

Conrad Aiken detested Mexico. From the outset, he eyed every-thing with disfavor and suspicion; referred to our streamlet as a "sewage outlet" (even envisioning a drama in which he'd saved Malcolm from drowning in it, a challenging feat if you were larger than a bug); sent Josefina for a river of liquor and bottled water; and deliberately bypassed the scenic to ferret out the sordid.

He delighted later in spinning images of unbounded decrepitude around our ménage, referring to a snarl of rags and tatters in which Malcolm supposedly "lived" on our veranda. Admittedly, our casita was no five-star hotel but neither was Malcolm Cinderella, nor I all the wicked stepsisters in one irritable witch-bitch and perpetually high-heeled bundle (my normal footwear being huaraches in which it is very difficult to clatter). Further obsessional nonsense erupted in his description of Malcolm's "really desperate condition," inflicted, I fear, by our difficult guest himself within a few days of his arrival, as he undermined all that had been precariously nurtured for months past.

But Aiken apart, we were beset with problems. It was now the rainy season, so it logically followed that our roof might leak. It did not logically follow that it would become a sieve, or that we'd find ourselves huddling beneath umbrellas while at meals. In spite of frantic inquiries, a repairman, hastily called, proved busily ineffectual.

Nor was this all. In one of his more inept moments, Don Pablo contrived to block our tiny irrigation stream so that, engorged, it surged throughout the house depositing muddy water laced with leaves. Compounding chaos, Malcolm's sciatica worsened and our two cats disappeared.

On June 10, one day prior to my birthday, Josefina tapped on my window at 5 A.M., beckoning urgently. I tiptoed through Malcolm's bedroom to the veranda to discover both cats returned but in extremis. Josefina was certain they'd been poisoned. It was too late to help. They expired within moments of each other.

I stared at the pathetic rags of fur, all that remained of our mischievous and loving pets, and sorrow laced with desperation overcame me. When Josefina suggested Pablo bury the poor relics I could only nod. But this precipitated an enormous quarrel with Malcolm. Still heavy with the previous night's liquor, he was furious I'd not summoned him to view our "sacred animals" before they were interred. In grief and rage he turned on me, half-sobbing. "You bitch!" he yelled.

Needless to say, our meals that day were difficult. Conrad and Malcolm did all the talking, the others never saying much anyhow, and I remember the luncheon discussion centering around the meager rewards for dedication. Admittedly one of America's finer talents, Conrad remarked with pardonable bitterness that he'd never earned over eight hundred dollars on any of his books. From this the subject somehow veered to the relaxing sexual mores which held, fallaciously, he insisted, that women's sexual needs could equal those of men.

"But we *do* have sexual needs and we *do* need sexual release just as men do," I interjected.

He glared at me. "You're talking nonsense!" he said harshly. "In fact, you don't know what the hell you *are* talking about!"

Aghast, I shut up. Obviously, I had flicked a nerve, but how could he insist upon this *schweinerei* before the woman whom he was about to wed?

Malcolm, unhappy, hung-over, and still angry, refused to intervene. I stared at him resentfully. Was it for this that I had banished Alan? That Malcolm might hoist drink for drink with this tormented man who could be as full of venom as an asp?

At any rate, I could neither take another month of Conrad nor of the Malcolm now constantly besotted. My need to get away became obsessive. That afternoon I studied a map of Mexico and noted Guanajuato, Guadalajara, Pátzcuaro, and Uruapan until the very syllables intoned a mantra; like the absconding father in *The Glass Menagerie,* I had fallen in love with Long Distance.

At breakfast I announced that I was leaving for ten days. Conrad looked stony; Malcolm, unsettled and withdrawn. When I left, hurrying to catch the bus, Josefina ran after me with a note Malc had slipped beneath my door which I had failed to notice.

Before the Flecha Roja bus could leave, Malc puffed up to my window, Conrad in tow, and handed me several pairs of tiny straw earrings shaped like sombreros. Costing a few centavos, they were popular with tourists; quite obviously, they'd been an afterthought.

"For your birthday," Malcolm said emotionally. I glanced at Conrad, that avid Greek chorus of one. "Thank you, Malcolm," I said, wanting terribly to cry and trying so hard to look impassive that I sounded remote and cold. "I won't be gone too long but I have to get away. I'll write you every day. Take care of yourself, please . . ."

The bus started up and we exchanged waving motions. Conrad took Malc's arm, turning him away, and so we moved apart. Aiken subsequently fantasized this scene: the little straw earrings metamorphosed into silver and were heartlessly rebuffed; I was off to "rendezvous" with that stable of lovers I had inexorably stashed in every corner of the Mexican republic, all panting to lure me with "wild parties and extravagant gifts."

But fate has an ironic sense of humor. It plays its practical jokes with exquisite precision. Conrad would have been grimly triumphant to learn that his fantasies about my "infidelities" were finally, if inadvertently, about to bloom.

I pulled out Malcolm's note. Couldn't we go to "a Rouen or a Chartres place soon and rediscover one another?" Our quarrels stemmed only from misunderstandings. We must, however, live alone once more although the ongoing responsibilities for such a house as ours had been unfair to me. As to his friends, he'd never again impose them . . . "they compel me, too, to an inimical uneasy rhythm." He urged me to get my own work in the mail "or else the old amour-propre will suffer," and signed the note "the husband of the rainbowpuss."

Reading and rereading the wistful tender lines, so evocative of the poet whom I loved, dissolved the acrimony of the recent days, and I began at last to cry.

Since the only train which would reach Guanajuato before midnight left at 7:10 A.M., I stayed over at the Canada. The ticket window next morning was monopolized by a *campesino,* an old peasant woman, shod in old automobile tires and laden with calabashes, endlessly haranguing the *boletero,* the much-harassed ticket-seller behind the ticket hatch. All the seats in second class were occupied by the time I boarded, but a kindly old woman offered me a make-do on her pile of serapes and mysterious small bundles.

We passed dun-colored hills inlaid like sand dunes with patches of scrub brush and the blazing gold and red of cactus flowers. An occasional cathedral rose like a white bone sentinel. Hills appeared furred with evergreens. A bird with a javelin tail skimmed past our window, then a herd of small white goats. Petrol tins from which spilled rainbowed zinnias banked the adobe shacks. At every stop, women ran alongside screaming: "*ay agua helada . . . tome agua helada . . . ay tortas de pollo, diez centavos . . . ay pina . . . una peseta . . . tome pulque, Señores?*" Some carried babies at the breast, pock marked or pox marked, arms shriveled or scabby and running. Girls had woven brilliant ribbons into their glossy braids. The whole car was eating goat cheese, tamales, hunks of meat and chiles. As we gathered speed, I noted a man in a sombrero and bright jacket perched in a tree, observing. Fences of organ cactus horizontally laced with bamboo fronds enclosed the small adobes. Young children suspended younger within *rebozos*. A truck bore the name HENRY in gilt letters above its windshield; another, GANGSTER. Vivid pink shirts dried on barbed-wire strands.

The *ferrocarril* stopped at every hamlet, and it took ten hours to reach Silao, where I changed trains. Now the scenery grew rockier and drier; the hills wore a poured and molten look. We saw more herds of goats. At a little after 6:30 we arrived at Guanajuato, a brown city, the color of baked mud. Its size surprised me. In the boom days of the silver mines it had housed 100,000, which had now shrunk to a mere 18,000 since only a handful of mines still operated, reworking ore discarded by the Spaniards. The train deposited me at the Plaza de la Union, and I settled at the nearby Gran Hotel Luna, once the palace of a governor, and set out to discover what I could of Guanajuato before dark. It proved forested with alleys, serpentine, cobbled, steep, replete with balconies and grilles and plazas, each with its round fountain, watertap, and decorative stone plaque. One was mysteriously dubbed Callejon del Beso (Kiss Alley) . . . And I envisioned presenting it, in a tiny geographical souffle, to Malcolm, as companion to his other favorite, Ruelle de la Demi-Lune.

In the darkening lanes I found myself among the genuinely medi-
eval: a street of steps, wide at its base but narrowing to a thread of stone
blocks as it mounted. Turning into one of these, I discovered an
abandoned playhouse—low-hanging balconies from which shawled
women watched me curiously, doorways opening apparently on nothing. From even smaller lanes, I could hear whispers of laughter and a
ghost of melody, and finally, at the very top, I emerged into a tiny plaza,
so minutely perfect it might have been the setting for a long-forgotten
opera. Around its obligatory fountain lounged half a dozen *Indios,*
serapes flung about them, cigarettes aglow. An occasional woman,
shawled against the oncoming night even to her nose, rested nearby. In
an open doorway I spied a cobbler working. From somewhere came
again a snatch of song.

This is bewitched, I thought. I don't belong here. The orchestra
will strike up; these mute figures will fling themselves into action; the
principals will enter, singing, and the audience will applaud.

It was dark when I returned to the Plaza de la Union. Señoritas were
promenading round and round the bandstand, always in one direction,
to the right, while the men circled in the opposite direction. I saw only
an occasional couple.

It had been wearyingly long, this day. Re-entering the Hotel Luna
I went straight to the bar for a drink and to write some letters. I had not
quite finished one of each when I was invited to join an American mine
manager and his Mexican friend, both engineers, middle aged, and
married. (At that time I considered anyone of forty middle aged.) We
drank Scotch, an unaccustomed luxury, after which they drove me
about the city, even more operatic by moonlight.

That night I wrote Malc about the trip thus far: that Guanajuato
was lovelier and far cheaper than Taxco; that it had a golf course where
he could again take up the game; and that I missed him dreadfully.

The following morning, a Sunday, the American went golfing but
Antonio, his Mexican *confrere*, offered to show me the countryside as
well as the Pantheon and the cathedral. So after lunch, drinks, and an
engaging drive, we headed for the Pantheon.

When I was about eight, mother had taken me to the Museum of Natural History in New York, where I'd seen the Egyptian mummies, an experience which so unnerved me that for months I could not sleep alone, the shriveled images rising before me constantly, but the grisly objects I beheld in Guanajuato were no Egyptian mummies, being neither embalmed nor swathed. By contrast, those which tormented me in childhood were models of neatness and decorum. After leaving Guanajuato, I made the following notes:

Whether due to the air, the clay, or chemistry, the dead in Guanajuato generally do not decay, they mummify. The rocky soil renders burial of any but the very tall imprudent. They are instead "stored" in a great courtyard of the Pantheon, bounded on all sides by walls of greenish stone, and filled from corner to corner with some thousand vaults. Most of these can be rented for only five-year periods, after which the previous inhabitants must make way for new. What is left is then conveyed through a heavy stone trap door near the rear of the courtyard and down a circular stone staircase, at the bottom of which lead left- and right-hand passages. That on the left, for those who have failed to mummify properly, connects with an eight-cubic-foot enclosure heaped with skulls and bones. The mummified, via the passage to the right, are placed upright in a long narrow room, one behind another, on a raised platform, an area near the door being reserved for children.

Some bear attached cards: "Beloved son [husband, whatever] of Emilia so-and-so." Through glass walls these horrors are all too visible. To some cling shreds of rags. Others are naked. All those I saw were shrunken, brown as petrified leather, wearing expressions of the purest horror on their sunken eyeless faces, mouths open as in a shriek. It left me with the most appalling interpretation of death, as though these ancient, woodlike shards had been overtaken at the moment of illumination by a torment so absolute, a revelation so hideous, it had rendered them as unalterably frozen in it as in amber.

"Before we go on to the cathedral," I told Antonio shakily, "I have simply got to have a drink. Or two. Or seventeen. I hadn't expected this." For once I could understand Malcolm's compulsion: he sometimes explained his peregrinations by claiming to have experienced unbearable apocalyptic visions. Well, I had just experienced mine, too. In spades.

When I came to I was in bed with Antonio. I did not just wake up—I'd quite obviously never been asleep—but it was as though all too suddenly a light had flashed, and with the light, awareness.

"Oh no!" I thought. "Oh, my God, no! What have I done now?" I had no idea where I was or whether it was night or day. I remembered only that we had started out to visit the cathedral.

I pulled away, sat up. Antonio looked surprised. *"Qué paso?"*

"My head," I said in Spanish, not knowing the Spanish word for hangover. He gave a cluck in sympathy.

I remembered a bit more about him. He was a mining engineer. Living in Oaxaca? Someplace like that. There had been an American with him when we met. "At least he's not here too," I thought savagely. *"Qué hora es ?"*

He continued to look surprised. Reaching, he picked up his watch from a night table. "Only eleven."

Eleven? P.M. then? I could remember nothing after four o'clock. Some seven hours had been totally obliterated.

The mummies—those I remembered. It would be years before they left me. And abruptly I remembered the man's name. Antonio Luna. How oddly studious he appeared as he lit two cigarettes. His clothes lay neatly folded across a nearby chair. I groped for comfort from this sign of the fastidious and accepted my cigarette automatically. Self-disgust numbed me.

With his free hand he cradled my head against him and kissed my shoulder. Had it been only yesterday I had left Mexico City? Only two days since Cuernavaca? "I must get back," I said, not knowing where "back" was.

He stroked my neck, affectionate, husbandly. But for my panic it might have brought me peace. *"Mi vida,"* Antonio said, low voiced and urgent now, but I grasped his hands with mine, like children in a willful struggling game, forcing us apart. All the old female fears, of pregnancy, infection, discovery, the outraged vengeance of a God defied, were floodlit with the superstition: *If I stop now, break it off now, right now, it will still be all right.*

He sighed but seemed to understand, for he let go of me and slipped from bed. His body looked white and thin beneath the deep tan of his face. Presently he emerged from the bathroom bearing a glass of water and a metal box. I was already out of bed and in my slip.

"Cafeaspirina?"

To save argument I took the aspirin. "Thank you so much," I said formally. "My head is killing me."

He, too, pulled on his clothes. "I will see you to your room. Will you have lunch with me before you leave tomorrow?"

"Of course," I said, grateful that he was understanding. Grateful, too, to learn I was after all in the hotel.

Back in my room, it was impossible to sleep. My guilt toward Malcolm bore no relation to this senseless lapse, to whatever had or perhaps had not occurred; rather for my every lack of understanding, each raging schism, our mutual refusals to accept less than the absolute from one another. I had to talk to Malc, tell him again how desperate was my need. I wanted to unburden, invoke his understanding and seek absolution, but this exposure to the dissecting arctic gaze of Conrad Aiken was a self-indulgence I could ill afford.

Whatever had occurred must remain aberration only, meaningless as a village glimpsed fleetingly at night from a train window. My miserable quarrel with Malc, the hideous Pantheon, an unremembered flood of alcohol—these had combined to produce the sorry denouement which memory had fastidiously buried. So at least I attempted to disarm the barbs which it had left.

Antonio and I lunched quietly next day, with no reference to the evening. Before he took me to the train, we exchanged addresses. Though we never met again, when I left Mexico that December, I notified him Malc would be coming to Oaxaca and asked him to watch out for him. And it was he who ultimately rescued Malcolm from the quagmire of the cantinas of Oaxaca and shepherded him to the relative, if only momentary, safety of the capital.

ᔐ ᔐ ᔐ

Uruapan (Place Where Flowers Bloom) was the lushest city I'd found in Mexico, with cascades and streams and rice and sugar cane, its cobbled streets lined with banana trees and coffee plants and ablaze with bougainvillea and roses.

The abortive experience in Guanajuato had so shaken me, I felt a continual need to communicate with Malcolm. From Uruapan I wrote to him three times.

> . . . I must tell you of a charming scene outside my window. It is pouring with rain, simply teeming, yet in the little round old-fashioned bandstand the orchestra is blaring away, a fey medley of Humperdinck-cum-Elgar-cum rhumba. There isn't a soul attending; Indians foot it unhappily among the drops, and a car or two dart past. But there sits the orchestra, there plays the orchestra, and its brass gleams merrily in the downpour. Now they're into Mozart.
>
> I'm at the Hotel Mirador recommended by Frances Toor in her Guide to Mexico, a very sweet room, two large beds, desk, balcony over the plaza, electric fan, bedlights, and the bath has tub, shower, and hot water. For this and meals I pay 5 pesos a night. This could be a fine replacement for the Hotel Somerset. I have just enjoyed one of the best dinners I've eaten in Mexico and in a charming dining room.
>
> Mexicans are totally vague about transportation. I wrote you about my train problems. Yesterday I opted to visit Chapala; the

schedule promised 1½ hours. It took 3 to reach the blasted place and 3 more to return, over a road so unspeakable it made the Acapulco-Iguala trail resemble the Pan-American Highway. I arrived back in Guadalajara with half an hour in which to pack and catch my train, which reached Pénjamo at one A.M. At six A.M. I was up again to catch the 7:25 to Ajuno where I changed to one leaving at 1:20 for Uruapan, due to arrive at 3:30 but not tootling in until an hour later. I now look and feel like an Aztec sacrifice.

But the most wearying part of the trip is over, apart from a 12-hour jaunt to Mexico City. The scenery from Ajuno to Uruapan was spectacular: true autumn colors, pine woods, valleys of deep red maples, in scenery rather like Majorca.

Much as I miss your dear company, this trip would have been altogether too exhausting for you, but do let's go to Veracruz when you are better. From there it's not far to Alvarado where Paul Strand's Redes was filmed.

Remember how you introduced me to the films of Eisenstein and Pudovkin et al. in New York? And how Davenport complained that with Russian films every time he woke up he saw a tractor?

I should arrive late Wednesday or early Thursday . . . I'll let you know. We can meet at Charlie's for a drink. And while in Mexico City I shall stop at the druggist for guess what?

My writing is becoming indecipherable. Next to you, mother, Paris, and New York, I most miss my typewriter. And so, dearest, to bed. I love you, your fineness, your brilliance, your helpfulness, and all the other things stronger than ourselves we have somehow created these last years without even altogether realizing it. All my love and dreams . . .

P.S.: "Hope Conrad and Ed are better. [They had both come down with dysentery and Burra was finally ordered back to the States by the doctor.] Give them and Mary my best.

Next day. Well the Mexican railroads have gone and done it again. There is only a single train to Pátzcuaro par jour, and it left at 1:10

instead of the scheduled 2:30, so here I am until tomorrow afternoon. I shall have to abort Pátzcuaro or Morelia to make up for it.

It is a très lourd afternoon full of a storm which hasn't broken yet which keeps me nervous and uneasy. I was so set on reaching Pátzcuaro and collecting mail and taking a further step towards you . . . I'm by no means as self-sufficient as I was; I depend so on your companionship and love and on your nearness. This is why I grow so desperate and angry when you can throw over these things which are so near and important to me, all in a second . . . oh let's go to Veracruz for a Rouen trip, a Mexican re-honeymoon!

Let's be as we were!

. . . At last it's raining. A flood. Tonight I am going to the theater since there's nothing else to do. *No Basta Ser Madre,* our old friend from Mexico City, here for one day. It should be very funny. Do you remember the little tent-show we saw in Oaxaca?

. . . Please get very tight several times and get that over with so we can have quiet and necessary talks next week. We can't discuss anything through jitters or a headache . . .

In Pátzcuaro I was beguiled by the butterfly nets of the fishermen in the street of the tea vendors . . . these set their tables, candle-lit, and serve canela, a tea mixed with alcohol, brewed in small braseros over a peaty fire. There are supposed to be mariachis, though I left too early to hear them . . . The festivities go on all night—very romantic. The tea reminds me of the brew Josefina brings us on cool mornings, orange leaves, very fragrant, with a dash of tequila added. A wonderful way to be waked up.

At Pátzcuaro I collected three letters and a card from Malcolm.

My own sweetheart . . . Your letters have been a joy to have. You sound very happy and I think the trip is doing you good. Do be careful, though. Don't rush around too quickly: and don't forget to take notes. It may smack of the journalistic but nevertheless to my

mind no account of memory or imagination can supply the gaps that
notes of the things which seemed to you vivid or graphic at the time
might have filled. I am trying to do a lot of work against your arrival
. . . afraid of this damned volcano going extinct on me . . . One of your
letters raised a lot of points we shall have to discuss; incidentally it
was a marvelous and dear letter; I think it's this typewriter that's
making me talk like an editor. However . . . you must get some things
out or else the old amour propre will suffer . . .

I cannot say how much I missed you and miss you. I love you
from the very bottom of my heart. We have a great rich life in front
of us. Well Godspeed and have a fine time, my—what is it?—
rainbowpuss, no what is it?—Mrs. Lowry . . . Your loving husband,
Malc.

He and Conrad had had a poetry session [the idea being to start at the
very beginning of all they had learned of troches and dactyls and the
ramifications of iambic pentameter], and had together evolved a
sonnet encompassing T. E. Brown, Wyndham Lewis, and Ezra
Pound, with, Malc claimed, most of the better lines being Conrad's.
On the fourteenth he wrote bitterly of the turn their relationship was
taking:

My dearest sweetheart: I am having a very dull time here without you.
Conrad is really not a friend at all though he pretends hard he is. He
is, in fact, a born chiseler of everything, of his friends and wives, and
of verses . . . Meantime as a gift horse, one has the sense of being not
only looked in the mouth but chiseled out of one's teeth as well . . .
You may be right about expecting too much. Still, one is always
surprised to receive less than nothing . . . For God's sake let's get
close together again . . .

The house goes well thanks to your prearrangements, though it
sadly misses you, as I do. I love you and long to travel with you again.
I cannot tell you how much I long for you in this Timon's environ-
ment of the distant and hostile.

Though you may be far geographically, you are nearer always nearer than anyone else, my tinfant . . .

Darling! Bright days in the middle of the rainy season! But they're all gloomy without you.

Conrad says his wedding papers will take longer to get through than he thought and has suggested taking a room uptown later. It is difficult to concur at this time without offense, but I think it's a good idea just the same. I'll wait for you though.

I think he's an extraordinarily evil person, capable of the profoundest harm to everything more human or with a more progressive nature than a cat . . . (the tender connotations of our sacred animal don't enter here). I mean the only thing he wouldn't harm is literally a cat.

He pretends to the deepest friendship for me, to admiration for my work, but secretly he is jealous, unreasoning, bitter, while the only real depth in our relationship is the extraordinary malicious extent of his hatred: but this is hatred for life, too: it is wretchedness become evil.

I am still playing the part of host but I can no longer bring myself to listen to the arid nonsense he talks.

Ed is at heart an arid and contemptible fellow . . . It is only our admiration for genius, even in its darker flights, that keeps me harboring such a person as Conrad under our roof. I set out to write of love, and have written, alas, of hate; but Jan, I love you, you are finer than all these people put together, you have more genius, more guts, only you must stick to one thing more, not disperse your fine talents, and you and I must at once simplify our lives and organize them alone . . . away from such evil friends as these. All my love, Malcolm.

On June 20 I wrote him from Patzcuaro:

Darling beloved of all the Mexicans and the Rainbowpuss: as soon as breakfast is over I am going to Janitzio about which Fenwick will tell you our friend Sr. Quigley once made a film. In the afternoon I shall snooze and it will rain and finally I shall go at night to see *The Merry Widow* with Maurice Chevalier.

I am newly armed with a small notebook like those we found in Acapulco to keep a fuller record of impressions as per your dear suggestion. Now incidentally I have some material which I believe will be of real use to you, in a minute way, with the *Volcano*. I'll tell you about it when I see you. [I was referring to the horrific mummies I had seen in Guanajuato. I would pass my observations on to Malc from time to time and he would share his with me.]

Missing you dreadfully last night, I decided a little walk might not be amiss. So out I went, garbed in my raincoat for warmth. Oh and oooh, what a dark city it is! I am a coward, I do believe, I trotted warily from our small plaza to the larger one, made a detour through this which was simply abysmal, and returned at an agitated lope, not breathing when a crimson serape lunged past me in the gloom, and collapsed in a state of maidenly relief when I was once more within the hotel portals. Very few people were about. Everyone was at the "box." If you had been with me it would have been very different, for we could have walked to all sorts of interesting places.

I went to Janitzio this morning as per schedule. It was a very obstinate day, cloudy and gray, threatening rain. I was accompanied by a one-legged Judas who was reading *El Machete,* the communist paper. The island is picturesque with its fishing nets hung to dry in what should have been sun. Venturesome, I climbed to the top of the statue of Morelos, so admired by Ed and Mary. It looks like an ad for a construction company—hideous isn't the word: it's the crudest possible parody of Diego Rivera.

I may skip Morelos on the advice of an American couple you'd like—Stanislavsky or some such name—they live in San Francisco where he is studying anthropology at the University of California. About our age, they were here a few years ago and say it was utterly different, the Indians as yet "unawakened," hence less hostile. I remember being told much the same about the nomadic Arabs of

North Africa four years ago: sort of the Noble Savage syndrome. You and I could enjoy it here however, take a lunch out on the lake at night, drink *canela* on the street of the tea vendors, ride through the *huertas* of Uruapan on horseback, wander together through the *callejónes* of Guanajuato . . . How I long for us! If it weren't that you're not yet well, I'd urge you to take a train and meet me here, but better to wait . . . We'll go next month to Veracruz and try to get off the beaten path to the north. Ask Fenwick about Papantla and the trip he made last month. Perhaps we could do something similar. Let us be very patient with each other too, dearest; let us try never to fret or get upset over trifles which cannot be helped.

Janitzio is a round island, very tiny, with a small fishing village girdling it, and a huge cathedral in the caves of which are idols likewise worshiped by the Tarascans who, by the way, speak little Spanish.

Houses here, as in Provence, in Italy, in oldest Spain, have the burnt brownish tiles and the burnt brown walls. We must go somewhere where we can smell the sea again.

I'm going out to find *The Merry Widow* before the rain spoils her plumage. Or mine. Be good. Be careful. Take care of yourself. There are the most gorgeous pusses in the hotel, each in a cage, Persian pusses: 4 large and 3 small kittens. But there isn't any *liebensvoll* rainbowpuss. (Please let's have lots of cats with long hair tied in blue bows.)

P. S. Monday A.M. Leaving this afternoon, spending the night at Morelia, and taking the early train or bus to Mexico City, arriving about ten. Home Wednesday the twenty-third in the afternoon. Two more days till I see you. Do you love me? Have you missed me? Will it please be good to have me back? Mee -oo-www-

The day I left Pátzcuaro there was another letter from Malcolm mailed June 18: "My darling . . . Had a letter from Fenwick inviting us both there—he's away again in a day or two, so accepted it immediately leaving the house in the hands of Conrad and Mary who were becoming

more or less unbearable. Ed is leaving, returning to the States. I have
no feeling for any of them: I hope they all choke, but all is peaceful on
the surface, the house is running itself. I thought the sulphur of the baths
at Cuautla healthier than the fumes of Conrad's mind: so here I am. I
am much better, incidentally, though the bus was hellish."

Fenwick, he reported, seemed in good form and Malcolm was
planning to spend a couple of days with him. He added that he had an
enormously renewed impulse to write which boded well for the future.
He hoped that I would not be too lonely on my travels, but hoped also
that I would get lonesome for him in the long nights on trains. Both he
and old Popo missed me.

Before leaving Pátzcuaro I wired him: "How long will you be in
Yautepec? If long enough, will go there first and return to Cuernavaca
with you. Write c/o Cervantes, 247 Paseo de la Reforma. Will call there.
I adore you. Best to F."

But when I reached Mexico City, the feathers had hit the fan. I
received an almost illegible letter from Malc:

My darling Jan: Here I am back in the old cow's horn [Cuernavaca]
again. Though not without a stormy passage.

Something pretty bad has hit Fenwick . . . He tried (1) to poison
me with petroleum. (2) to burn down the hut I slept in. (3) To kill
me with my stick. He has refused to give over half my things including
Ultramarine, etc. He is really *crazy* by now: for instance he climbed
up on the roof and started howling like a dog. I confronted him
frankly with the fact of V. D. and he burst into tears, threw books at
me, his typewriter off the table, etc.

It is true he was decent to us. So is Piddledeepom, the old
parish dog.

[The second page must have been enclosed inadvertently
because here he was totally incoherent and the raving phrases,
evidently meant for Fenwick, are violent, bitter, and totally incom-
prehensible. There was also this postcard, addressed to me in
Mexico but enclosed in the letter:]

Salud y pesetas y tiempo para gastarlas. What this means I don't
know . . . Well I don't know and do know at the same time. Anyhow
I can't tell you in this postcard what the trouble is . . . I cannot believe
that what has happened to the poor fellow has happened at all . . . it
puts him in another light, a bad one. All love, Malcolm.

Keep this postcard: a masterpiece.

I couldn't help feeling sorry for Fenwick: he'd had no idea what he
was letting himself in for. Though I did not for one moment believe that
he was "by now in the nut house," he would obviously belong to the
past tense for us both. Malcolm's letters throughout my trip had
revealed so openly the man I loved and treasured that it was hard to
accept that the man to whom I was returning might be the same man
from whom I'd parted in frozen silence on my birthday. What had
occurred in Yautepec? When and why had he decided to revisit Cuautla
now that there was no Alan to hustle him away?

I returned to Cuernavaca depressed and apprehensive.

We had lost Ed during my absence. Mary had painted a few delicate
floral water colors. Conrad and Malc had held literary jam sessions, but
Malc had accomplished little since Conrad's arrival and was in decidedly
worse shape. The sciatica which had crippled him had not worsened,
though his back remained troublesome, but on the increasingly numerous
mornings when he could not function without a drink, he was too shaky
to raise a glass to his lips without employing a towel as pulley. Draping a
towel around his neck, he would grasp one end in his left hand, wrap the
other around a glass held in his right, and pulling down on the towel with
his left hand, manage to elevate the glass to reach his lips. He was quite
proud of this unhappy performance which, since I had to pass through
his room to enter or leave my own, I witnessed on too many occasions.

He would drink anything. I had thrown out the rubbing alcohol I'd
used to massage his back, but he gulped the contents of a bottle he
thought contained hair tonic but which Josefina had refilled with
cooking oil. We were extremely careful to secure anything that might
be dangerous, and I had long since trashed the Cuautla Veronal.

When I had a few free moments I wrote Peak, wanting his gentle, generous and nonjudgmental wisdom. "The serpent in Eden," I told him,

is a very little one but poisonous nonetheless. It is the cook, who has gradually come to feel she owns the house, Malcolm, myself, her own time, and any change she feels like lifting from the market money. If I discharge her I must, by law, pay her three months' wages, and since we don't expect to remain here longer than that, it would mean paying two servants for the balance of our stay. Besides, her replacement might be worse. But when it comes, as it did this weekend, to having your housekeeper march truculently around your guests and bang the dishes on the table, the serpent in Eden is whirring his rattles . . . (her rattles?) . . . and Eden appears less lovely and more like a garden in dire need, with grass too long, with paths unswept, with sulky volcanoes on the horizon just flexing for their next eruption.

I suppose what I'd like is someone soft and quiet, silken and suave, moving on padded feet, speaking in a small squeak, and robbing me, if the need be imperative, in an imperceptible and discreet fashion. (I think I have just described Dr. Fu Manchu . . .)

You could live in this country a hundred years and swell with lethargy, and grow fat and soft where your brain was, and watch butterflies the size of swallows, white, and swimming with the air, and listen to the lazy snip-snip of the gardener's shears. New York is a dream far away in another time. The world is something one reads of in the paper, if and when one even reads the paper. Time becomes nonexistent and day and night blend without significance. One could be a king in a place like this. One sometimes is.

I miss you yet there is no sense of lack or loss since I go on talking to you in the same way as in times past, times yet to come . . .

One day Don Pablo approached me about Josefina's birthday. In celebration, he desired to make *pulque curado:* would the Senor and I permit and sponsor (i.e., pay for) this? *Pulque curado* can be made with various fruits—pineapples, strawberries, peaches, berries; it was the strawberries he would recommend. Since *pulque* to me had always tasted like liquid Uneeda Biscuits and came from fly-encrusted vats, I had strong reservations, strawberries or not, but Josefina deserved our recognition, whatever form it took.

With the Aiken ménage in residence, she was flooded with fresh demands: at hours which were not her market time she must expect to be dispatched for *habanero* and/or bottled water, while her cooking, marketing, and housework more than doubled. (To give Aiken his due, he at least paid for the *habanero*.) So we not only agreed to enliven Josefina's birthday, but gifted her as well with silk stockings, her favorite extravagance.

I had to admit that strawberries improved the Uneeda Biscuits mightily. Conrad and Mary were in town consulting their *abogado*, and Malc, after a tentative sampling of the pinkish sludge decided to rendezvous instead with his slumbering *Volcano*. Pablo and Juana and Josefina finished the *pulque* with scant help from me, and our ex-bartender and his lady then peeled off to return the empty barrels.

Emulating Malcolm, I tried to immerse myself in work, but a leak had developed above the table which I used as desk. My first doubts as to the wisdom of our celebration struck when I sought out Pablo, whose chores now included dealing with the roof, and found no trace of him. I consulted Josefina.

"*Y Don Pablo, Jose, dónde está?*"

She shrugged and made her tippling gesture. "Where would he be? In the pulqueria with the Juana! A woman, to enter such a place! You should speak to her, Señora."

"We need him now," I told her. "You'd better go and find him."

"Yo, no, Señora! I do not enter such a place." Outraged virtue and jealousy tightened the muscles of her jaw.

"Well stand outside it then and yell for him." It sounded like an order and it was.

"*Como le gusta usted, Señora,*" she muttered sulkily. Needless to say she ignored me and remained in her kitchen, banging things about.

I tried to return to the entanglements of the Varsity but the leak, though small, was steady and I could not concentrate. Where was Pablo?

Conrad and Mary returned toward suppertime. The rains had gradually ceased, and we sat on the long veranda sipping our drinks, smoking, and talking fitfully. As always after the rains, the air was fresh and fragrant. We conversed in low voices, gazing beyond the pool, beyond the slow slopes of the land to the *barranca,* beyond the gorge to the emerging lights of Amatitlán, and further still to Popocatepetl and Ixtaccihuatl, faint and lovely against the twilit skies. It was that time of evening which blends and magnifies distant sounds: a neighing horse with threads of music and the scraping noises of those insects to whom the night belongs.

Suddenly around the corner of the house arose the sounds of running feet and without warning Don Pablo erupted onto the veranda, his breath rattling, his clothes stained and muddy, his back and arms glistening with what might have been rain or sweat. "Look at his shirt," Malc whispered sharply, and I caught my breath at the sight of smears which looked dreadfully like blood.

"Madre de Dios!" Josefina breathed behind us. I had heard her enter but her crackling Mexican Spanish bubbled as she pelted him with questions.

It seemed that in the *pulqueria* Juana had flirted with a soldier. They'd both been laughing until Don Pablo slapped her. When she ran into the street, he followed, caught her, and slashed her until she fell. Then he began to run.

"The *policía,*" he pleaded now when he could catch his breath. "You have not seen me, patron; if they come here you have not seen me! Only give me a few pesos, por favor. You will take them from my pay."

Malc, fishing in his pockets, produced some change. Josefina dashed to the kitchen, returning with tortillas wrapped in newsprint. Shaking uncontrollably, Pablo snatched at them, leaped over the veranda railing, and plunged toward the barranca. We watched him go in silence. Malc was the first to speak.

"We certainly have the damndest luck with gardeners," he remarked gloomily.

Josefina plucked at my sleeve. "The lantern, Señora, you ought not to let him take the lantern."

"What did she say?" Malc interrupted. "What is she talking about?"

"It's about that lantern we bought him a while back. She thinks he might come back for it."

"Why? Why would he take that chance?" Mary asked.

"Forget the lantern," Malcolm said. "What are we going to do about another gardener?"

"Can we have dinner now?" Aiken demanded. "We're absolutely starving."

Deliberately we did not speak of Juana. It was as though the opening of that door would commit us all irrevocably to Pablo's act.

Josefina, with her nose for news, collected conflicting stories. First, Juana was dead. Then she was not yet dead but dying. Finally she had been *como los muertos*, but was recovering. Her head had been shaved; Pablo had slashed at her skull and across her flirtatious mouth. She remained in the hospital some weeks. The *policía* did not come. They made no inquiries of us. They appeared to show no interest in Pablo. And so one morning he returned, to take a job in, of all places, another *pulqueria*. He felt secure again.

At long last July 7 was upon us—Conrad's wedding day. We dressed for the occasion, Malc in a suit and tie, I in my city clothes. Conrad took a final snapshot of us; Malc, badly needing a drink, appeared morose; I looked remote . . . the sun was blinding me. Happily for Conrad, it was the worst picture I had ever taken.

While we waited for their final cab, an odd emotion hit me and my eyes welled up with tears. I noticed Conrad's fleeting expression of surprise. Momentarily, I felt bereaved and suddenly very sorry to see them go.

No sooner had the cab bearing them away turned from our drive into Calle Humboldt than Malcolm, without meeting my glance, announced with the false heartiness which always accompanied this phrase, "Well, I guess I'll go uptown." Mephisto had left us but not his siren song.

That afternoon, I wrote to mother: ". . . Mary is an artist, cultured and kind, just right for Conrad. It is his third marriage but I believe this one should last. They seem genuinely fond of one another.

"We gave Conrad a bottle of Irish whiskey and Mary some blown-glass animals as wedding gifts. There was no chance to celebrate; they rushed off immediately, eager to put their affairs in order and leave for Europe. They were too broke to see much of Mexico but Conrad disliked the little that he saw: I think its lushness affronted his tidy Brahmin soul."

That was putting it mildly. With all the handicrafts available, Conrad selected but a single item to take with him: a ceramic representation of a turd, life sized, which he exhibited with enormous glee.

Since we were still without a gardener, we had made frantic inquiries, and in this wise there appeared one morning a tiny gnomelike man with doggish eyes and a pitiable sweetness. His name was Hilibierto, and his need was grave. His wife, equally gentle and doe-eyed, was soon to bear their child. Emotions scattering, we hired him on the spot. That same afternoon he moved in.

He seemed too good to be true. He worked assiduously, spoke in respectful tones, even to Josefina, tended his own affairs, and did not drink. His Maria did not flirt. True, the garden was never quite well watered, the grass never adequately trimmed, and he planted corn surreptitiously among our roses, but his air of boundless goodness and honor impugned mistrust.

One day Don Pablo visited Juana in the hospital and she forgave him. She even promised she would take him back, but when he visited her again the police arrested him, moving not swiftly but in mysterious ways. Don Pablo was now in the penitentiary.

Gradually the pattern of our lives resumed its old tranquillity. Malcolm was hard at work on *Under the Volcano,* while I typed his revisions. His sciatica receding, we attempted moderate excursions. And then one morning a fresh problem arose: he had difficulty urinating. Our local medico, pointing to six boozy weeks with Conrad as the probable cause, prescribed pills which stained his urine bright orange but at least enabled him to pass it.

On July 31 I again wrote Señora Baldwin: ". . . the garden suffered severely last night in a hailstorm, if you can call it that. The hailstones were the size of mothballs and pelted straight into the kitchen through the tiles. As to the garden, that they beat to pieces. It looked as though we'd had another plague of ants . . . Hilibierto was busy all day cleaning up but it is once more reasonably respectable. He is intelligent: there is neither difficulty nor undue friendliness between him and Josefina."

Late in July, Maria bore his child in an abandoned house. A midwife attended the long and difficult birth which produced a baby girl. There in that candle-lit room we visited them and their first-born. "They look like an engraving of the holy family," Malcolm said reverently.

August started with a week in Mexico City. We saw the Laughtons in *Rembrandt* and attended a concert at the Bellas Artes, but mostly we bought books, some in French, and quite a few in Spanish, for we'd been taking lessons. The books turned out to be a godsend: no sooner were we home than Malcolm fell ill with malaria. I piled blankets on him for the chills which alternated with his bouts of fever.

He'd written me of one such siege while he was in Torquay, though a later letter from his father indicated that at that time he'd actually been drying out. Whether his illness now was due to ever-present mosquitoes, lowered resistance, alcoholic excesses, or an actual recurrence was indeterminate, the doctor favoring all of the above.

To me was entrusted the dicey task of giving Malc injections, the doctor providing a hypodermic needle and a vial of medication. Thank God he was a capable instructor for I'd heard horror stories of fatal consequences from air bubbles. Meticulously, I boiled the syringe and administered injections and *poco a poco* Malcolm's symptoms eased. In a few weeks he was strong enough to resume work on *Under the Volcano*, though he'd lost forty pounds. Throughout his illness he remained gentle, funny, and appreciative. Our closeness and the unity disrupted so by Conrad, even as Malcolm's health, seemed to be on the mend.

I'd written Peak of our improved relationship and he answered me at once: "Jan, why did you tear up the 'very long letter'? If it said substantially what your last letter did I should have liked to have read it . . . it would be a longer happiness. You know, I almost pray you will find your way back together whenever one of you starts on another path. I am so sure you would both be leaving, if leave either of you ever did, something more valuable than 'peace, moderation, steadfastness.' . . . I want to make that something shine for you some day, in words perhaps, as it shines for me. It is enough that you are contented at the moment. I feel like writing on tiptoe with lullabies dripping from my pen . . .

"Your letters are a source of life to me . . . I believe I value them more than any letters I have ever received. I am looking forward both to your letters and to Malc's poems with great eagerness . . ."

∾ ∾ ∾

Later that month Hilibierto brought us a chicken. Barely half-grown, it was mostly bones and russet feathers and a perky, canary-like cheep. It was too young to kill, and we let it run about the garden, pecking and scratching and peering inquisitively about. We became fond of it and privately determined to keep it as a pet. At night it slept with Josefina in her room.

It was running about now as we left the house for Malcolm's first excursion since his convalescence. The piece of cloth tied to its leg dragged behind it, and every so often it bent its swift head and pecked viciously at the knot. Seeing it now, Josefina looked about for Hilibierto. "Don Pablo, Don Pablo," she called forgetfully, perumptory and wheedling. "Tie up the pollito before you go. To the little tree."

"'sta bien," Hilibierto responded. He was watering the zinnias, taller than any zinnias have a right to grow, holding our poor patched hose contemptuously between his hands. It was his great aversion. Every week he begged for a new *manguera,* and every week I wrote to the *dueña de la casa.*

It was now half past three, the date, September 9. As the rainy season neared its close, the weather would become more English, fresh, sunless, and cool. Until November 1, Josefina predicted; until *Los Muertos*. By November 1 we'd have been in Mexico one year.

An odd trio, we talked together as we walked, my Spanish swift though incorrect, Malcolm's more labored but more accurate. We held hands as we walked and conversed in English, which Josefina felt scant compunction about interrupting. We were to visit Pablo at the "Peni," and had planned to buy him cigarettes at the nearby *tienda* till we found it closed.

"Another one who likes his *pulque!*" Josefina tossed her head contemptuously. "*Quien sabe* if the *tienda* by the peni will be closed *tambien?*"

"Oh I don't think so. It's visiting day after all. What cigarillos does he smoke?"

Her full skirts swung from side to side, the little snub nose, which lent her face a childish look, wrinkled in concentration. "I think Alas, I think it is Alas that he smokes, Señora."

"I expect conversation is going to be tough going," Malcolm said. "We can't very well ask him how he likes it there. Or can we? But it's impossible to understand him anyhow."

"For the *santo* of the Senor it is necessary to make *mole poblana*," Josefina interrupted. "With *guajolote.*"

"That's awfully rich," I told her. "The Señor's been quite ill."

The Señor was glaring at us both.

"But Señor, for his *santo*," Josefina protested. "*Guajolote con mole* for his *santo*, Senora."

"His *santo* is a year off. That is, he has no *santo*. Only a birthday."

"*Como, Señora, no santo?* And you have no *santo* also? How is it that in your country there are no *santos?*"

"God *damn* it! Really now!" Malcolm exploded in disgust.

I tried to explain that to non-Catholics there are no saint's days, but it was not a subject in which I was well-versed. I let it peter out though she remained filled with wonder at our heathen state. *"El pobre Señor, no santo! Pues, qué cosa! Qué calamidad!"*

But the matter passed from her thoughts as she spied an open *tienda* where we found Pablo's cigarettes. Leaving it, we climbed a pebbly road which slid beneath out feet. Concerned for Malc, I grasped his arm. "You okay, darling? You want to rest a bit?"

"God, no! It feels great to be out and moving after lying about like a decaying vegetable."

"Estamos aqui," announced Josefina presently.

The penitentiary, a large and quite new building, was located in Acapantzingo on the outskirts of Cuernavaca. Within its gates, soldiers in ill-fitting uniforms approximated guard-duty or strolled about chewing gum and picking at their teeth. No two seemed garbed alike: some wore khaki; others, green; still others, gray or a washed-out shade which might once have been blue. Footwear varied similarly, comprising boots, shoes, huaraches and, in one case, puttees. The rifles they bore were likewise of undetermined sizes, shapes, and vintages, united only by a general appearance of neglect. I had been told Mexican ammunition could be uncertain: one shell might contain only traces of gunpowder, while the charge in another could be doubled. It had a deleterious effect on rifle barrels and personnel alike.

We passed without difficulty through three entrances and half a dozen guards. Once past the final gate we entered a small room where a woman attendant ran her hands over Josefina's body. She was very thorough, and both she and Josefina giggled throughout the process. They waved us by when we offered ourselves to the procedure. We found them extraordinarily polite considering our appearance: Malcolm in splotched gray flannel bags and I in a tired and somewhat rump-sprung knit. We had sought to avoid the Lord and Lady Bountiful appearance and I must say we succeeded.

An iron gate admitted us to a large quadrangle bounded on the right by prison walls and on the left by a wall roofed to a depth of half a dozen feet along which sprawled a melange of prisoners and their visitors. At its far end was a basketball board and hoop. Nothing conformed to my preconceived ideas of a prison yard. Men lounged in small groups, joking and laughing; one strummed at a guitar. To the nearest Josefina called: "Wishes *mi patron* to see Don Pablo . . . Pablo . . ." Her face crinkled in thought: she had forgotten Pablo's surname. "What's he called, Señora?"

"Gonzalez?" I supplied uncertainly.

After ogling us, the man disappeared round a protrusion and we heard him calling. When he returned it was with Pablo and Juana. Pablo looked well but no less shiftless than when he'd tackled gardening; Juana seemed drawn and thinner, her cropped hair growing out, but the scar from nose to lip still very plain.

"*Buenos tardes, Señor, Señora.*" Pablo smiled, making a cursory motion toward his forehead. "Here I am, eh?" He laughed, his Juana smiled, their discomfiture infectious. We essayed grins.

"*Entonces,* here they have you, Don Pablo, shut in like a great *puerco, verdad?*" Josefina's humor, though forthright, was never tactful.

"We brought you cigarettes," Malcolm interposed. Pablo's gaze shifted from us to the ground to the proffered gift.

"*Gracias, mi patron. Pues,* the worst is I don't know for how long. 'Tomorrow,' they tell me. Or 'We haven't had time to think about it.'" He scraped the dirt with the toe of one huarache, shrugging his palms upward. He was learning to weave belts but silk here was *muy caro,* twice the price of silk in Mexico City. He spoke about it with the grave concern of a *comerciante.* Presently, in the manner of one reminding himself belatedly of the obligations of a host, he showed us round the peni. The far side of the prison structure was bounded by a wall topped with half a dozen strands of barbed wire and beyond this extended corn fields planted and tended by the prisoners. The wall was very low and the barbed wire strands were far apart.

"Good God!" Malcolm exclaimed. "Doesn't anyone ever escape?" Only at the entry gates had we noted guards.

"A woman escaped from the women's prison last week," Pablo offered. He did not know how or why or whether she'd been captured.

To a question from Malc, he disclosed that 180 men slept in dormitory rooms where lights burned constantly. Nights were, of course, the worst.

A man with a kind and patient face approached. He brought us a little carved wood and silver monkey on a string, which was very ugly. Nevertheless we bought it for 50 centavos without bargaining; it was something he had made. Later we worried lest we had been disloyal, but Pablo had completed only half a belt. Still, to atone, we promised him silk from Mexico City.

In a kind of corridor along one courtyard wall lounged those to whom no visitors had come. Their faces revealed only the defeated wariness of the dispossessed. "A woman tried to smuggle marijuana to her *esposo*." Pablo continued. "They have given her five years."

"Five years!" echoed Josefina, who loved gossip. "*En el distrito federal* a woman had her hair done in big curls . . . each held a marijuana cigarette for her *amante*." She chuckled happily and winked at Juana. "But they caught her. *El amor cuesta mucho, verdad.*" She changed the subject. "Do they feed you well?"

He made a gesture of friendly contempt. "Coffee and bread for *desayuno*. Lunch is a few tortillas, some frijoles or a little meat, the most *corriente*. Nights, coffee and bread again. You don't die on it."

We returned to his mat, declining cigarettes from the supply we'd brought. He would make a belt for me but I must bring him silk from Mexico City. "But two colors, Senora, *sabe usted*. One color is not interesting and three are not pretty. It is two that are right." I favored three myself, but no matter: I would bring the silk.

Malcolm asked why he did not learn carpentry, which was likewise taught. Pablo, shrugging, grinned and wiped his nose with the backs of two fingers. He was learning arithmetic. It was so difficult. He had no time for more.

We asked about his fellow-inmates: that chap who had just passed, rolling by like a sea-farer: who was he? "He is a chauffeur. But he ran over someone."

"And that good looking man with the beautiful girl with pale eyes?"

He wasn't sure "But probably he had killed somebody." He referred to murder in an off-hand way and pointed to a mild-looking older man who was sitting with two children. "They gave him five years," said Pablo. But if he killed again it might be ten. "It is easy to escape but we are not badly off," said Pablo. "Besides, if they catch you it goes worse afterwards." His smile broadened as he added, "Sometimes they send a man on an errand and he returns next day. But he usually returns. For some it's not so bad you see."

A bell sounded and one by one the men arose. Those without visitors were already moving toward the building. Pablo collected his belongings, his mat, his serape, his two fiber bags with fruit and cigarettes and the half-finished belt. Smiling, he shook our hands and Juana's; they did not embrace. "Hasta Domingo," Juana told him.

"Hasta Domingo . . . Come again soon, *patron*,"

At the gate, Malc took my arm and pointed to a tower with searchlights we'd not noticed from the quadrangle. "See, it's not so easy to escape after all."

Once in the street a man on horseback nearly ran us down. Josefina flared with rage. "Mira, Mira" she shrieked. "Uno es tan animal que l'otro!" The man reined and yelled back and a crop of insults spurted from both sides. Gradually Josefina, like a ruffled hen, settled and smoothed her feathers. "Aie, Señora, the poor Pablo, shut up so, like an animal. It is better outside, *verdad?*"

After our farewells to Juana, she grew silent and preoccupied. Only once did she turn to me. "You must not forget the little gift of silk for Pablo. When you go next to Mexico, *verdad?* If you wish, I can take it to him."

Malcolm was silent too. Presently he paused to light his pipe. "You know," he told me between puffs, "I believe I know why Pablo smiled so much."

I played it straight. "Why *did* he smile so much?"

"Well, figure it for yourself: at one blow, literally, he got rid of all his problems . . . the ants, the floods, the scorpions, the pool, and us. Not such a bad day's work." He grinned at me.

"He nearly got rid of Juana too," I pointed out.

"Yes, but when you consider . . ."

"Señora, we really must do something special for the Señor's *santo*, Josefina interrupted. "Even if he doesn't have one."

"Oh bloody hell," said Malc, but he was laughing.

～ ～ ～

During his convalescence, propped up on a serape-covered couch on the veranda, he'd repeated to me the story of Paul's suicide, reliving his own role. It was always the same story: Both were drinking and Paul was talking suicide. Malc, agreeing he'd be better off in the next world, then helped Paul seal the windows with newspapers. Leaving, his final words to Paul were, "Now go do it!"

It was midmorning, the air sweet smelling from the previous night's rain. To the east, the magical volcanoes glittered in the sun, while below our parapet papaya and black-skinned zapote trees were richly hung with fruit. Josefina's atonal version of *"Tu ya no sirve como mujer"* drifted from the adjoining dining room where rhythmic thumping announced that she was ironing.

Why was it so important for Malc to retell the story of Paul's suicide? Could this be perhaps a reason for his nightmarish binges? I wanted to disbelieve his tale but there was in his recounting a quality I could not dismiss. There was so much about Malcolm I could never know. Beneath each layer he permitted me to penetrate lay further, deeper layers. So many Malcolms. How many had I known? How many could anybody know? How many might lie forever unexplored?

Following our visit to the peni, Malcolm, in better shape than for months past, suggested one to Mexico City, where our joy in each other's bodies seemed reborn. In every way that week was among our happiest. One night, after seeing Anatol Litvak's film *Mayerling*, we wandered through the city's streets and back to the hotel for a night to rival August 10, 1934, at Martha's Vineyard.

Much later I would watch an orange tree in my small orchard approach its final days, its branches brown and dry, its curled leaves yellowing, but prior to its passing it was spectacular. Hundreds of oranges covered every inch of bough, small but so very sweet, as though this final burst of gold must atone for all the crops it could never again bear. It resembled a tree in a Chinese watercolor and I wanted to weep for it.

So it was with our bountiful, passionate week in Mexico City, for there would be no more.

In the predawn of October 6, foreshadowing as an omen, Cuernavaca was rocked by an earthquake violent enough to tumble us from bed. The house swayed and crackled, and I had a nightmarish vision of scorpions raining from the tiles. We crawled to the veranda from which, in the ominous reddish glow which lit the sky, we could discern our pool, rocking and sloshing like a boat adrift. From many directions arose the faint outcries of animals, burros, cocks, and dogs, all blending in the sounds of protest. At the far end of the veranda we saw Josefina, crouched in fear, and as the shaking eased we joined her.

"Aie, Señores, que temblor!"

The seismic violence quickly passed but the gods were not yet through.

꙳   ꙳   ꙳

With no warning, there appeared on our doorstep one afternoon two people, elegantly boned, supremely confident, triumphantly British, and bristling with charm. Ara and Arthur Calder-Marshall were surely two of the most beautiful people of their world, and I should like to have been able to remember them that way.

In England, where Arthur had known Malcolm, he had published several novels and a volume of stories. Now on a contract with MGM, he and his wife had driven from California and were staying at the Cuernavaca Inn.

In the book *Malcolm Lowry Remembered,* there's a chapter from Calder-Marshall saying that when they visited Cuernavaca they found us living in total squalor. He also alleged we were bored with one another and I carping and dissatisfied with Malcolm's failure to publish as facilely as Arthur. Nothing can have been further from the truth. Arthur was that poisonous troublemaker who had had the good fortune to have been born beautiful. *Externally.*

So I did *not* greet them "barefoot and blinking in the light," as Arthur claimed (like some small rodent emerging from its lair?). We were not, after all, inhabiting a burrow. And to go barefoot in Mexico with its teeming insect life would have been as witless as Arthur's other oft-repeated favorite, Malc's tale of falling on top of me in Spain. Nor did I subsequently approach hysteria when Malcolm pawned our cheap alarm clock, by then, surely, the least of all my problems. In Arthur's fanciful recounting, our 30-foot veranda shrank to an area barely large enough to accommodate four people, with "railing eaten away by ants;" our pool was not only tiny but "matted with dead insects," our picturesque Mexican street became a pock-marked unkempt alleyway, and I am referred to as a "Jewess from the Bronx . . . discontented, ambitious, bored," and unhappy that Malc was less successful than the golden one (Arthur himself, no less, who would no doubt have been startled to learn that I shared Malcolm's opinion of his talent as distinctly minor).

But all this pales beside the fatal blow they dealt us. When Malcolm greeted them, rosy and vigorous, he spoke proudly of his recent and hard-won sobriety. Having known him in England, Arthur certainly knew how alcohol affected him. I could only hope that their next words were not uttered out of malice, for they slyly responded, "May we have a drink?" (They have stated that my agreement to meet them in a cantina was condescending; nothing so elementary: it was despair.)

I suppose in the long run it might have made no difference. Had they not shown up when they did, there were others who could have substituted. So at that point, all unaware of the numerous distortions which would later surface, I responded to their charm and beauty and thought Ara gorgeous, lusty, and outrageous. At their urging we introduced them to the local cantina where Malc duly lived up to expectation by consuming drink after drink. Defeated, I left them there to their carousing.

The next day I found a scrawled and barely decipherable note from Malcolm. ". . . Janny . . . A nightmare of insomnia taking the mind . . . am trying to walk it off, will probably go to Cuernavaca Inn for breakfast emphasize definitely nothing *destructive* in this or against your own wishes.

"I love you. If I am a fiend I am a nice fiend. Will ring you up—not before you are through sleeping, whatever that is. You are the nicest beautiful woman I ever saw in spite of me, Malcolm."

So began once again the too-familiar pattern: Malc returning briefly at odd hours. The fragile resumption of our interdependent days in the Somerset and our good weeks before and after Conrad lay once again in shards. That week I wrote to Peak:

Old friend: I'm going to write you an uncheerful letter. Do you mind terribly? It is, of course, about Malcolm and myself. I did not delude myself so far as to believe that I was entering upon a carefree existence when Malcolm and I left New York last September, over a year ago. It has been a difficult summer as you know, difficulties inherent in us both and not to be ignored. Malcolm possesses a powerful impulse to destroy what he most loves. Some pitiless heritage infuses him: happiness becomes the cross he can least bear. A guilt fastens upon the simplest enjoyment and he tears down all we've worked to build. Malcolm could stand at a threshold, the choice of retaining me on one hand, his demon on the other, and he would follow where it led for he has a will to suffer. Even more than he needs me, he needs to lose me for the supreme pain of yearning. He has written me over and over that he wishes I might be ailing, even maimed, so that he could "comfort" me, or in peril, that he might fight for me; over and over he has written he would die for me.

But to live for me is too difficult. And there is always within him
the child's need to test . . . "if you love me you will bear this; put up
with that; endure, endure, endure." Always the deeper probing, the
broader demands, the insistence upon further proof. In surface ways
he has changed since our marriage, but underneath, not a hair's
breadth. At times there is a tenderness in him so vast I can sink into
it as into prayer. Yet there is also this torment so pitiless it could kill
us both . . .

. . . So I live always, now, on edge. Malcolm is like the sea: he
pulls me to him, then pushes me away, that he may once more draw
me back. It is a wearying tide . . . .

As the days passed and the Calder-Marshalls lingered, Malcolm
continued to drink heavily. The cork was fully out of the bottle now
and my life in Cuernavaca had become a squirrel-cage. Unable and
unwilling to drink myself into oblivion with Malcolm, I turned to my
old standby: travel.

Since we'd been haunted by *Redes,* photographed in Alvarado by
the incomparable Karl Freund, I endeavored, though without success,
to persuade Malc to visit the locale with me. It has been imaginatively
reported that when he refused, I pranced off with the consul who was
our next-door neighbor, this absurdity thus becoming the basis for
much inept speculation: Aiken endowing the gentleman with British
nationality; the Calder-Marshalls preferring to think of him as French;
while one befuddled biographer shrugged off the question with the
comment that there seemed no way to determine who was right. The
answer is simple: neither.

Our neighbor was an American vice-consul whom I was not to meet
till mid-November, a lofty gentleman, thoroughly fed up with what he
considered a drunken hooligan next door and most punctilious about
avoiding both of us.

As I did not thus flagrantly depart in mid-October with the then-
unknown, neither did I do so in a white sharkskin suit and "red high

heels," if only for the valid reason I had never owned them. But even had I been possessed of such a jauntily impractical outfit, I should hardly have elected to wander the by-roads of Mexico decked out like Tennessee Williams' Blanche Dubois. But I did head off to Veracruz alone.

I spent Wednesday at Cholula, where churches cluster like mushrooms. My favorite was the Church of Los Remedios, built atop a pyramid dedicated to Quetzalcoatl, the plumed serpent. Beneath it lie stairways and passageways from preconquest civilizations. In the church itself, a sign proclaimed: *"Desea Usted Besar A La Santissima Virgen Toque El Timbre"*—roughly translated as "If you want to kiss the Virgin ring the bell."

After Veracruz, I proceeded to Los Cocos, where I boarded the "wagon" for Alvarado, which, prepared as I was by *Redes,* I found delightful. A Spanish-Indian fishing village from a bygone century, bounded by the sea, the Alvarado River, and the bay. Sand dunes formed a backdrop to the port. The area was rife with palms.

But there were no letters from Malcolm on this trip and, increasingly uneasy, I cut short my stay.

It was late afternoon when I arrived back at Calle Humboldt, the date, October 27. The cab pulled up the drive, and as I neared the entry I saw Josefina, her mother, Balbina, four of her children, and her sister, Trinidad, all in the dining room, roosting like apprehensive owls. It spelled disaster and my first thought was of Malcolm.

"Good God," I greeted them. "What on earth is happening?"

"Aie, Señora," said Josefina sullenly, "I don't know how to tell you. The house has been robbed."

I dashed through the rooms while the assemblage followed, keening, *"Todos, todos!"* And it was true. Typewriters, camera, all my clothes (including those from Paris, and my Harris Tweed coat), serapes, floor mats, sheets, and towels . . . everything was gone. All that remained were books and papers and those garments of Malc's too grungy and bedraggled from their recurring baptisms in the long procession of cantinas.

"Y el Senor?" I asked, although I knew the answer. Josefina replied with her tippling gesture.

The Calder-Marshalls in at least one biography are quoted as stating flatly that nothing had been stolen. Perhaps the same myopia which led Arthur to describe our 30-foot veranda as hardly large enough to accommodate four people and our pool as matted with dead insects was still at work. I tried to call them but, the turmoil having no doubt lost amusement value, the golden pair had moved along.

Malcolm had not come home at all. Hilibierto was spending nights now with his wife and baby. So Josefina had stayed with her own family, leaving the place abandoned. My urgent letter to Señora Baldwin brought a swift reply.

Dear Mrs. Lowry: I was so distressed to hear the news of the robbery, but cannot understand how it happened with two servants around the house. Never be too sure of them. Did you have the police investigate the whereabouts of the maid and the gardener? . . . Your letter sounds most upset . . . if you would like to trade places we can install you here and go up there until you are ready to leave. The expenses here are minimum, no gardener, the place is watered in three minutes (so small), no phone and no need of it. We use gasoline lanterns with very small expense and our water is good . . . and free, so far. You would only have to pay 100 pesos rent but no outside expenses that turn into money . . .

Malc had become unreachable. I would find him in tiny hole-in-the-wall wineshops at six in the morning, or on a bench in the plaza, or not find him at all until he drifted back to our gutted house. He was, of course, vaguely aware of the robbery and seemed to believe he had personally been responsible for salvaging our disordered manuscripts. And he was far from ready to renounce his alcoholic pilgrimages.

As to the Señora's offer, the prospect of a small inaccessible dwelling on an Acapulco alp, with neither telephone nor electricity, horrified me. Acapulco itself was still relatively remote, and these factors considered in the light of Malcolm's proclivities rendered any such isolation the very last thing I could cope with. It would have amounted to interment.

For I was at long last coming to grips with the realities of my life. I had to find a job, and no longer could I afford to disregard my options. I had no clothes nor any money for a new wardrobe. I had to have a job, something to avoid being, as Blanche Dubois says, "dependent upon the kindness of strangers." For my self-respect I had to be earning my own money.

New York was one possibility, but there was no one there to whom I could turn for work. As for Hollywood, I knew I'd get short shrift from John (Davenport) or Arthur (Calder-Marshall). There was, however, Donald Friede, who had once offered aid. He had now started a script agency in Hollywood. To Malcolm, this might seem anathema, but for me it was a matter of self-preservation. The barriers between us were expanding ominously, and I was growing numb. How much longer could I stumble from crisis into crisis? Or drift blindly on an intolerable current?

I wrote to Donald.

Chaos now compounded chaos. Hilibierto gave in his notice and told the police that the thief was Josefina. Though they arrested her, they shortly let her go; there was no outward evidence of guilt. Furious at the indignity, she flounced back to the house and packed her things. Before she left, she spat out that Hilibierto was himself the culprit. Her look was meaningful. "And Señora, I could have told you things," she said, banging down the path. Whatever she might have been or done, I was sorry to see her leave. She had helped me through so many crises—a starchy lady, a survivor, and a great source of material.

Malcolm then took off for Mexico City. I still had bills to pay, books to pack and ship, and the house to turn over to Señora Baldwin's Mr. Hodgkins, so I would meet Malcolm later at the Hotel Canada.

And now, at last, I encountered the famous vice consul. Having heard of our robbery through Bernardino, he phoned to introduce himself. His offer of aid was curiously belated. When I said I would be leaving the next day for the capital, he offered to drive me in and I saw no reason to decline.

Our short association ended when he dropped me at the hotel. So much, alas, for a flaming rendezvous in Veracruz with an exotic Frenchman!

Struggling to maintain some echo of accord, Malcolm and I achieved now only intermittent flashes of our intimacy. Night after night he escaped into the bars. Mornings, too many mornings, I would routinely reclaim from the hotel desk whatever he had pledged. Requests that they curtail these advances met with no success; doubtless they were afraid of scenes. Then came the pivotal communication which provided me my option: Donald responded to my letter. Would I be interested in collaborating on scripts at his Hollywood agency? I wrote for further details and for the first time revealed to Malcolm that I was considering this course. It was after supper and I was readying for bed.

Malcolm's response was to seize my shoulders, march me to the door, and thrust me bodily into the hall. That done, he locked me out and ignored my alarmed protests. Shocked, frightened, and embarrassed, I found myself clad only in a slip in the hotel corridor on a wintry night. There was nothing for it but to descend to the front desk, try to ignore some very astonished stares, and obtain another room. We must, I reflected bitterly, be constructing quite a legend.

On the following evening I found another of Malcolm's penciled notes.

Darling:

Of the few pesos I had all have been taken either good-naturedly or otherwise. They will not serve me downstairs without my paying. Therefore I can get nothing to eat. There are other and worse things that may be pending. I do ask if possible that my father not be informed. In spite of everything I have a great love for him. The shortest way out of this room is via Veronal tablets or the window, though doubtless my way will be barred downstairs. Anyhow, if I come back again I have already informed you that there is the window.

There are many worse things than drink and Mexican officialdom is one of them.

Why I should be treated like this when I am perfectly sober and my money has been stolen in this hotel among other places perhaps I shall find out soon. I shall have my revenge, however. During these days I have been principally one thing: in the most ghastly invintigeable [sic] despair. I say invintigeable because as yet I think it is.

I love you too, but too much to want you to put up with me as I am. And it isn't all my fault. It is either eight or nine and I cannot wait any longer. You do not indeed seem to be coming back . . . I am trying to think of the most obvious place where you might be and that is Butch's Manhattan. There I shall be absolutely without funds altogether. It is not too cheap but I shall certainly choose what is cheapest . . .

Drink, if it be known, though still a problem—is one of the slightest of them . . . It must be obvious that this could not have been written by a drunken man anyway.

The truth is, bread or wine, whatever, that the only problem, the only legislation on any human or inhuman being, fair or foul, is money . . . It has taken me a long time to realize what a corrupt world it is that permits this . . .

I keep hearing your steps but they are not your steps. I have already said that I keep hearing your steps but they aren't. And I can't wait any longer. And since they won't serve me here, I prefer the door to the window.

Butch's, then, where I must be till you come . . . Malcolm.

For me the episode had clarified one thing: drink was far from "the slightest of our problems," and Malcolm was, indeed, "invintigeable." My only immediate option seemed to be Hollywood, and I so wrote Donald.

During our final days we were both totally depressed, but Malcolm was angry, too. Unable to accept the idea of separation, we wrestled back and forth. Then came the night of November 25.

I have described the evening in "Not With A Bang" which appeared in *Story* in 1946. I had turned in early, and unable to sleep had sat up reading *Yama*. Malcolm had stumbled in at one o'clock that morning and out again at seven. When the door opened now it was to admit a pair of bellboys supporting Malcolm between them. He drew himself up and flung them off with affronted dignity. As they bowed, half-mocking, and departed, he stalked over and sat heavily on my bed.

"Just a proper tin Jesus, aren't you?" he announced. He had been holding his jacket bunched up on one side; now he drew it apart and laid a finger on his lips. "You must be very quiet. It's asleep."

I felt the stirring of alarm. "What is it? What have you got there, Malcolm?"

Opening the jacket, he laid on the bed beside me a small black and white puppy. "A man on the street was selling it. I bought it for you."

The puppy started to sniff about the bed and suddenly planted its four small legs more firmly. I snatched it up and dropped it on the floor.

"It's such a little, little dog," Malc said, rebuking me.

"It isn't a question of size. I have to sleep in this bed. You practically never do."

"You are a bitch," he told me violently. He picked up the puppy and held it in his arms. "It's everything I have in the world to love," he said.

I was starting to cry inside, wanting his nearness and his tenderness, but he wouldn't give me that. The dog was a symbol: This gentle, innocent, helpless creature is your husband, Malcolm. Look after it and mop up after it and cherish it and give it your protection.

He struggled to his feet, bundling the puppy back inside his jacket, swaying a little. "I love you," he told me with excessive firmness. "God damn it, how I love you because you are a wonderful woman. I am not doing anything destructive. If you would only understand that I am not doing anything destructive."

He made his way uncertainly toward the door. I was clouded with pity for him and his little dog, and for both of us. "Malcolm, don't go. We'll keep the dog. Don't go." He didn't answer. He pulled the door wide open, teetered on his heels, then strode into the hall, slamming the door upon me on my seat of judgment.

The next morning I borrowed the hotel typewriter and wrote:

My darling, for you are my darling no matter what has passed between us . . . Can't we wash away the bitter memories of these recent weeks and find each other as so many times before?

If only you could believe in yourself as I in my heart believe in you! You have the finest talent of any writer today and when you told me you will live when Calder-Marshall and I and others like us are forgotten and out of print, you were absolutely right. You will, but you need help and I *can* help you.

You tell me I don't love you, that it is too late. Oh Malcolm, don't let it end like this. There is something in you stronger than your love for me but there is love there too. I know there is love there too . . .

↬ ↬ ↬

"Well, are you coming to Oaxaca with me or are you not?" Malcolm demanded coldly. He'd barely glanced at my letter.

"Malcolm, don't *push* me, please."

"Oh for God's sake!" he exploded. "Never mind, God damn it. Never mind! Go to Hollywood! Play with the billygoats and their long fat cocks! Go ahead! Go! And the sooner you go the better!"

. . . *this is the way the world ends* . . . Wretched and helpless, we glared at one another.

"If you'll excuse me," I said when I could speak, "I'd like to use the phone. There was an ad . . . someone who wants a passenger for Los Angeles . . ."

"Then call him," Malcolm shouted hoarsely. "Tell him you'll share his room while you are about it. That ought to bring things up!"

I could have slapped him but I was afraid he'd slap me back. It was not a Shakespearean farewell.

Before leaving Mexico, I gave Malcolm's passport and papers into the keeping of our friends the Millers, lest he lose them. (Later on, he did.) And since Marcia and Alfred Miller were hosting a young American likewise Oaxaca-bound, I arranged through them that he accompany Malc. His name was Harry Mensch. Wounded while fighting with the Spanish Loyalists, he was seeking to regain his health. (As it turned out, Malc nearly finished him.)

On November 28, roughly 13 months from the date of our arrival, I left Mexico. The young doctor whose ad I'd answered called for me at the Canada. Malcolm, his face as stricken as my own, carried my bag to the car and is reported to have later described my departure as "accompanied by two American friends." Confabulation to the last.

I've tried not to give a one-sided picture of our life together. Obviously, had Malcolm been no more than a troublesome drunk I'd neither have married him nor remained his wife throughout four stormy years. Our good periods, fragmented though they were, were irreverent and gay. We were children together in a secret garden, for Malcolm, sober, could be brilliant, rollicking, and irresistible. Together, we had had so much: freedom to work without restraint, to travel when and as we wished, and to explore our love. But it had never been enough.

"My God! What shall I do without my misery?"

Finale

The lunatic, the lover and the poet,
Are of the imagination all compact.

—Shakespeare,
A Midsummer Night's Dream,
Act 5, Scene 1

Scratch a lover and find a foe.
We have lingered in the chambers of the sea
By sea-girls wreathed with seaweed red and brown
Till human voices wake us, and we drown.

—T.S. Eliot, from
"The Lovesong of J. Alfred Prufrock"

I had to make a decision: either I was going to be a part of Malc's life totally, or I had to become independent. To be the wife of a drunkard meant that more and more I would be drinking with him and more and more sharing his peregrinations, and more and more I would thus be destroyed. That was not what I wanted. For this I was not ready. I owed something to my background, to do better, to respect, if you will, my heritage.

So began the final phase of our correspondence, tragically different from that which had governed our courtship. There was bitterness in many of Malcolm's letters, inevitably engendered by my association with Donald Friede, businesslike though this was to remain. Donald had proved a friend when I had needed one, but Malcolm could see only lovers in my friendships, past or present. In my letter of December 9, I tried again to cope with this.

My own dearest: Lunched with Davvy [John Davenport] and the Calder-Marshalls yesterday. Clement [Davenport] was indisposed and did not join us. I saw her for a few moments. She seems gentler than last year. They live now on Schuyler Drive in a much more imposing house though I personally prefer the pretty Spanish on El Contento.

I have taken a room at fifteen dollars a month for the time being. You need not, I repeat, not worry about my relationship with D. He has been very decent. I have told him quite frankly how I feel about you and he has replied, with equal frankness, that he could never offer what you have given me. It is to be a working partnership and nothing more.

Actually, he is infatuated with Patricia Ellis, a young actress, very outgoing and friendly. He was madly in love with Jean Harlow before her death, which devastated him Had she lived, he believes they would have married.

No word from you as yet. I worry about you constantly. Where are you? How are you? How is Volcano coming? Your silence frightens me. Living without you is only half a life. My dearest darlingest, please write!

Guard your manuscripts, and as you finish them, send them to me and I'll retype as needed and submit them. When do you leave Mexico? . . .

In a few days I wrote to him again but more days passed without a word. Then, at 7:49 on the morning of December 15 I received this wire:

MALCOLM WENT TO OAXACA SAME AFTERNOON WAS QUITE ALL RIGHT THEN STOP STAYING AT HOTEL FRANCIA HARRY WRITES MALCOLM IS NOW IN BAD CONDITION KEEPS DRINKING LIKE FISH BUT NO USE YOUR WORRYING AM SURE HE NEEDS NO MONEY, BEST WISHES, ALFRED [MILLER].

And this was followed by a letter from Marcia, his wife, informing me that Malcolm was in jail! I wired him 20 dollars and a message, "For God's sake what is happening? Am totally distracted by your silence." Any ill-founded hope I might have harbored that leaving him could inch him toward sobriety now crashed, the maelstrom engulfing me as well.

John Davenport was still working for MGM in Hollywood, and I had contacted him and Clement when I first arrived there. But he was soon to return to England, leaving behind some fairly hefty debts. At the only soiree at the Davenports' which I attended, a blowzy woman confronted me and announce in stentorian tones: "I hear your husband is in jail!" Whether John or Arthur had broadcast Malcolm's plight, I thought it cruel and tasteless.

The following week my first letter from Malc arrived, headed: "In the stir . . ." He claimed he'd been jailed because his papers had been left with Alfred; because he'd been mistaken for another; subjected to the third degree; confined to a bare cell with cutthroats and a child; and all for mysterious "political reasons not yet clear." Had he again bragged of flying for the Loyalists or voiced his fantasies about enlisting in the International Brigade?

Typically, he described the ordeal as a "fantastic experience," though bitterly convinced someone would steal it, or it would remain unpublished, or even, he asserted cryptically, be "mutilated" like *Under the Volcano* while in his suitcase. The crying of a small goat somewhere seemed to be myself pleading with him. He bemoaned the terrifying things forever befalling us and longed for us to come together once more as we had in Paris. Then, with the bitterness which would become recurrent, he added that the thought of me "in the arms of that paunchy Harpo Marx or worse" was more than he could stand.

A few days later I received his second letter. Out on bail, he found Harry had had all his clothes cleaned, and for the first time since I'd bought him his blue suit, the waistcoat fitted. "When you said sadly that all my clothes had a history intimately connected with us and I looked round the room, I felt there to be something so overwhelmingly sad about our separation forever . . . I felt the very presence of our first love in the room . . . The blue jersey you gave me for a birthday present in 1934 . . . your little green jersey I got you at Austin Reed's before I came to Paris . . . my tweed suit which we saved up for in July 1935 . . . the shirts Trinidad made . . . the other shirts you bought me on Broadway in the winter of '35 and which still serve as if brand new; all these things which had been so ragged and dirty and which were now so spruce seemed to be conspiring to say, even if you replace us, we write the history of your marriage, don't let that go . . . if that goes, all else good in your life goes with it . . . it cannot be true we shall never meet in Paris on New Year's Day again and ride through the snow in a taxi; and the clothes say 'no, it cannot be true . . . you will meet again and love as never before.'

"What shall I do? Which way?"

But hard on this letter followed one from Marcia:

. . . I am terribly sorry I can't send you any good news about Malc, but I think I should tell you the truth. He's been drunk ever since. And about two weeks ago he was jailed. Harry sent for his papers. We sent down those we thought were necessary. Again today I received a letter from a young woman who also went down there for her health and who's a friend of Harry. He's in jail again. A ten-peso fine or ten days. She stated frankly that she didn't like to forward the money since Malc is drunk and may not remember debts he incurs, but toward the end of the note she says she'll do it anyway and get him out. Also, she and Harry asked for our advice as to what to do.

Malc's been telling everyone that Harry's a Communist and that Harry better leave town or someone will shoot him. The entire thing sounds like an awful mess to me, and to be quite honest I don't know what to advise under the circumstances. Harry will probably go to Guadalajara. He says Malc's been quite a task to him, and he feels he'll not get better if he hangs around saloons just to accompany Malc. I realize it's not a pretty picture I'm painting, but it's the truth as far as I can get from Harry's letters.

By now I was settled in Hollywood and working as a script assistant at Donald Friede's agency. It was not arduous work, and it gave me an income of my own; I was no longer dependent on Malcolm. There were also new friends to meet, including some of Donald's like the brilliant composer of *Ballet méchanique,* George Antheil and his wife, Boske. Of course I was still in touch with our friends in Mexico and receiving news of Malcolm from time to time, and had not yet come to believe that our marriage was over. After all, we were still man and wife, and were still writing to one another as such.

On December 22 I wrote Malc again.

At last some news! I only wish it might be less disturbing. As to your papers, I left them with the Millers so they might be safe: we lived in Mexico a year with no need for presenting them . . . Plainly, those problems which beset us are still present. I cannot envision replaying these last bedeviled months. To make a habit of such misery is unthinkable. We need breathing room and signs on both our parts that we are gaining in maturity. Nor do I at all appreciate your snide envisioning of me "in the arms of that paunchy Harpo Marx" ad nauseam. My life here is a quiet one. It is long past the time to cease torturing us both. My relationship with D., as I have assured and reassured you, is and remains on a totally business level. I had to find work and he offered it and that is all!

I know you've not sought my opinion, but if I were you I should head for New York where you'd have Whit and Martha and Matson and Ann W. to advise you on Volcano.

Met today with D. and Eleanor McGary, who was Von Sternberg's assistant. She asked how you and Von S. compared. Donald said you had far more genius, far more value as an artist, far less security. We then spoke of contacts, of cultivating those with influence, and I admitted we'd been too casual in this regard, but D. demurred. "When you have as much talent as Malcolm, you don't have to bother with anyone. If he works consistently enough, that will speak for him. Malcolm doesn't need contacts in order to get ahead. He doesn't need anything. Only hard work.

On December 29, having no further word from him, I wrote a long letter which began: "A strange evening. I am feeling 'disassembled,' as though all my moves in life have been controlled by an invisible player, even that I am but part of the dream of a restless sleeper. *'Que toda la vida es sueno y los suenos sueno son.'* However I am not lonely because I work damned hard and I work damned hard because otherwise I would be damned lonely. For God's sake, *write!*"

And then, also on December 29, I received a wire from Malcolm from Oaxaca: "ALL LETTERS ARRIVED TOO LATE. IN ANGUISH ABOUT EVERYTHING. HELP, LOVE YOU. S.O.S. COME OAXACA."

I felt I'd swallowed a time bomb. At dinner with Donald F. and Patricia Ellis that evening, I thought I was handling myself well, all things considered, until Donald told me, "I'm going to have to send you home."

"Why? What's the matter?"

"You're ruining the evening, that's what's the matter. Your tension is affecting all of us. Go home and take a sedative and try to regain control before tomorrow." He held my coat, excused himself to Pat, and put me in a cab.

He was quite right, of course. I was like a piece of glass on the edge of a high ledge, trembling at the least vibration. Since I had never been able to do anything with Malcolm drunk, how could I hope to do anything with him now, even supposing I could scrounge up the fare to join him? I sent a tormented wire to Peak, and a panicky wire to Malc, and a plea to Antonio Luna to try to determine what was really happening.

On January 5, I wrote again. The week had been a nightmare. "My love, my love . . . do you remember tomorrow? It is our anniversary. Yesterday I received word of you which brought only despair. Without you I feel brittle as coral, small pieces snapping off forever tumbled in a gray indifferent tide . . ." (In *Volcano,* Malc excerpted portions of my letter with the caustic query: "had Yvonne been reading Héloise and Abélard?" Always befuddled about my letters, scanned boozily and left behind in bars, small wonder he reconstructed their contents so haphazardly.)

In response he wrote that the agony was not his "poor fault," that he could not explain "because of one thing or another," but that if I ever wished to see him alive again I must come to Oaxaca . . . he was in anguish.

I sent an immediate two-page letter to the British Consulate-General in Mexico City, urging their investigation of Malcolm's situation and requesting they communicate their findings to me with all speed. In reply I received a correct, formal and starchy note, consenting to ask the brother of one of their staff, who resided in Oaxaca, to advise them of the facts but whether or not he did I never learned.

From Antonio, however, I received a letter-card dated February 10: "Dear Jan . . . Your letter received . . . I had to come to Mexico City and your husband came with me. I left him at the Hotel Canada last night. I am going back to Oaxaca today and will write you soon. Malcolm intends to go to the States but he does not say where. Best wishes, Antonio." Considering what the trip with Malcolm must have entailed, the note was a model of restraint. I do not recall that I ever heard from him again.

On February 12, I received another desperate wire from Malc, complaining that Antonio broke promises, Harry was a phony, and Alfred had grown preoccupied. Our sole hope lay with me. He would, of course, forward my fare to Mexico but did not know where to send it. The wire closed, "Darling, darling, darling said the Chinese nightingale."

Panicking afresh, I again wrote the British Consulate urging them to persuade Malcolm to enter the British Hospital for treatment as well as to forestall continued threats of suicide. I added that though I was sure of Arthur Lowry's cooperation, for Malcolm's sake I hesitated to inform him of his son's condition. In response, the Consulate informed me crisply that since Malcolm had categorically refused to call on them they could offer nothing further (further than what?), but that they were forwarding a copy of their reply to Lowry senior. A door hitherto closed was thereupon flung wide.

In the following days I received several letters from Malcolm, now afraid to approach a doctor preparatory to applying for an entry permit, because he could no longer estimate the needful amount of alcohol to down to conceal the knowledge that he was "next door to insanity" and actually unfit to travel anywhere. But by God, Harry was a phony, and Alfred, too. He consigned all of them to damnation! Somewhat offhand-edly he added that money problems would resolve themselves once we were again together. And besides, his money hadn't arrived anyhow and when it did, it was impounded, so what the hell?

A further letter turned on me as well. All my letters were contradic-tory; one said go to Laredo; another, England; a third, San Antonio. Would I for God's sake tell him what I wanted! His money was messed up "through no fault of my own, and then, again through no fault of my own, I needed most of it for reasons I can explain later."

I grew more and more convinced Malcolm did not even read my letters; why on earth would I want him in Laredo? Or in San Antonio? But obfuscation was by now a too familiar pattern.

On discovering that the British Consulate was making inquiries, Malc fled to Acapulco in company with an oddly allied pair: David W., a scrounger we'd met during our first weeks in Mexico, in current tandem with Gilda Gray, an aging headliner whose swirling hips had swiveled her to fame.

Malc's February 18 letter to me announced bluntly that our tragedy, our real tragedy, lay in our difficulties in communicating. My information was inaccurate; my news, directions, addresses were all totally confusing. He had returned to his earlier obsession with the American Express, convinced that I was hiding my true whereabouts. Given my role of the eternal suspect, it was now Donald who replaced Dicky and David and Gardner and Lord knows who-all else. Interspersed with protestations of his deep love and affection were accusations that he had wanted all along to go to Acapulco and that I had practically forced him to select Oaxaca even though he had "prayed and pleaded with you after my last illness . . . if I didn't get to the seaside somewhere I would crack up."

It was an odd accusation. When I left Mexico he was not in chains, and furthermore it was he who had elected Oaxaca for reasons to do with *Volcano,* but for Malcolm it was ever easier to accuse than to utter for one moment mea culpa.

He then returned to the subject of money, reiterating that "after all you were getting 25 bucks a week from that blight and God knows what more"—plus, much that went in fines, and 400 pesos stolen on the Oaxaca train, and never knowing my address properly, and his mail being impounded, all these factors had "inhibited me from sending you so much as a centavo." And, as of this writing "we are all perfectly broke here and I won't be able to even send you your fare supposing you decided to come."

Then he adds, interestingly enough in the light of much later events, that they are living in a shack they built themselves on the beach

. . . (shades of Dollarton, his future Canadian paradise) . . . and literally foraging for themselves as well. It would, he adds, do me good too, and he suggests I borrow the money somewhere, because as soon as we were reunited "the financial thing will as you know solve itself." And even if "you had to rough it till March 1, what of it?"

As to my "perpetually confusing instructions," it was becoming ever clearer that there could be few handier explanations for Malc's drowning his sorrows than a wayward and unreachable wife cannily concealing both her whereabouts and peccadilloes. No matter that my every letter contained the same address (that of my 15-dollar room), befuddlement served Malcolm well. Whatever might transpire would lie forever "outside of my control," and remain "not my poor fault."

But just as I was reaching these conclusions, another beautiful, poetic letter came: sun, sea, and air were giving me back to him and oh, God, did I remember Martha's Vineyard? He added that such monies of his as were neither stolen nor impounded, he'd gambled away "in a frantic effort to get enough to send you," adding pathetically that in spite of everything, I'd find good reason to be proud of him throughout our months of nightmare.

His next letter apologizes for his jealousy and mourns our sweet lost songs: the "tippet mouse" song, and "no work has been done by the little Cat," (though much is being done by the Big Cat on *In Ballast*).

I too faced problems. Donald Friede's agency, where I had been working since my arrival in California, had not lived up to expectations and its demise was imminent. I wrote Malc, advising him that barring a miracle I'd be leaving for New York. Meanwhile I broached the subject of psychoanalysis: "Menninger has just published *Man Against Himself,* a book we should both read, dealing with the will to die and the varied forms it takes: alcoholism is one. There are destructive depths in all of us; these last months, years, have loosed far too much chaos on us both.

"If we could only meet as friends instead of adversaries, develop tolerance and trust, and learn to laugh at things we've quarreled about, perhaps in some lovely simple place such as Carmel or that visionary South of France we never reached . . . with nondestructive friends,

friends to us both, become again Pupdog and Rainbowpuss . . ." But we had been apart almost three months and all that time Malc had remained besotted.

On March 4, Arthur Osborne Lowry contacted me. His letter, though brief, was friendly. Would I write his Liverpool address enlightening him as to Malcolm's state. His motives were most kindly; my answer would be "held in confidence."

My reply covered three single-spaced pages detailing numerous aspects of our life and problems while in Mexico, soft-pedaling alcohol. To protect Malcolm I did not reveal his episodes in jail but stressed his need for competent analysis. "With Malc," I wrote, "drinking is his escape from a world he cannot face. Worries about his interaction with that world and, above all, about his work, trigger a need for such escape; alcohol brings an illusion of security.

"He has true genius, more than all but a handful of living writers, but until he has learned to face life and the world, this may never fully be developed. Malc has honesty and gentleness and a potentially enormous strength of character, but he has real need of security in order to function. Not only financial security, which you have provided for him, but inner assurance. He has no defenses. Where many sensitive people establish a shield against the world, Malcolm takes the world head-on, and is hurt.

"He loves and respects you deeply . . . he wants your praise and your encouragement . . . your kind letters to him have been greatly cherished. May I beg that in his present precarious mental state you do not chide or scold him in any way, for it might have dangerous results. I know you will understand that I do not mean to be presumptuous, but as Malcolm is now, so much more can be accomplished by constructive criticism . . ."

A few days later I received a snippy letter from David, the soldier-of-fortune, informing me Malcolm had explained in detail how all his problems were directly of my making and proclaiming that in just three days he'd restored Malc to total health, only to lose this edge when I failed to rush back to Mexico.

This had become a more-than-twice-told tale. Everyone who knew Malc, myself included, had at one time or another become inevitably convinced that his/her/their insightful ministrations had/could/would have wrought miracles but, alas, given enough time, disillusionment and weariness would follow. That disillusionment was not one-sided, a further letter from Malcolm made clear: his companions had absconded with his cash, which had, of course, been intended for me solely, and he'd had to return to the capital "without a penny." Their address, however, was American Express, Los Angeles, so no doubt I would retrieve the debt and "give them hell."

He added he was ill with "some colitis or other, kept collapsing," but was all right, "absolutely on the watercart," and drinking only tea and occasionally cider. He kept hearing my voice, seeing my face, believing himself once more in our old apartment in Paris. "You have done everything to pull us together. Don't give way now. All my love and again love my pusscat. Pupdog."

Meantime, letters from Arthur Lowry were arriving. One, dated April 9, written to let me know he was sailing for Egypt on business and wished to "remove any anxiety" that my letter to him had gone astray, and let me know that it had been accepted "in the spirit in which it is written," and would be treated with all confidence. I had been brave and dutiful in writing it, for we had a mutual and sacred confidence in a matter causing us both "much agony of mind." He closed "with my best love, Your affectionate Dad." I was extremely touched.

His second letter, dated the fourteenth, was less encouraging. He would continue Malc's allowance for the present, but the first step was that we must return to one another. Next, Malc must drop his "undesirable companions," and "cut out drink." When I should write him this had been accomplished, Malc would find in him "the father he has always had." He added Malc must realize that should he but do as his father desired all would be well. Malc's difficulty, as he saw it, was his habit of "going his own way and opposing his father's." Reversing this would do more good than "all the psychology in the world," which had only the effect of covering up Malc's folly and creating "a neurotic outlook." He closed by saying "I rely upon your own excellent influence to bring him to his right senses. Shall await further news from you. With my best love, Your affectionate Dad."

It was a kind and well-meaning letter and totally misdirected. All of Malc's problems arose because of opposition to his father's will? Not without some truth, perhaps, but any damage was long since done. The critical issue now was how to minimize it. Though he could not have foreseen this, Arthur Lowry's letter produced exactly the opposite effect of that intended. There was no way for me to oblige him in what he requested of me; I had already tried and tried to bring Malcolm to his senses and had failed notably.

> ❧ ❧ ❧

When Donald's agency finally collapsed, I was not left stranded but, through the timely intercession of a fellow agent went to work as Jimmy Stewart's secretary. In time I would add other film stars as well. The flexible hours provided opportunities to write.

When he heard that I was working as a Hollywood secretary, Malcolm complained that the work would overshadow my life and I would never develop as a writer. That may have been true enough, though later I did publish several stories based on my life with Malcolm in Mexico. But working with Jimmy Stewart, and later with Olivia de Havilland and Carole Landis, brought me into contact with a side of life I would never have known otherwise. Replying to fan letters, sending out masses of Christmas cards—such work could be boring—but sharing the lives of such famous individuals was absorbing in itself, and I was more and more frequently meeting other celebrities of the world's film capital. I could have written a book about *that* period of my life, but, of course, it would not have been a book Malcolm would necessarily have approved of. Perhaps the way I looked at my new life suggests that I was changing as a person. No doubt I was. I had trained as an actress and perhaps Hollywood brought me back closer to the career I had intended to follow in the first place.

It was now time for me to leave my single room, and I moved to a little two-room house at 1135 1/2 North Larrabee, just off the Sunset Strip. It was an engaging neighborhood, though my quaint and woodsy little home with its huge fieldstone fireplace and paneled bookshelved walls has long since been swallowed by apartments. As my companion, I acquired a long-haired tortoise-shell cat whose eyes the director Ruben Mamoulian once described as "lamps." I named her Jezebel, after the film and especially after Bette Davis.

For some time Malcolm's letters had been growing fewer and more scattered. One of the last reached me in early May. Circumstances, he wrote, had made a return to the States impossible. He was again in Acapulco, but this time with "real friends" who would help us. It was "mostly bunk" about malaria there, but even if true there certainly worse things in Hollywood, "where your very soul will rot." He deplored my new occupation as "a doleful thing to do" which would frustrate my ambitions and do nothing toward achieving the independence for which I'd wished and to which I was entitled. But I must act if we were to be saved: we were "at our last gasp as you well know."

He would *not* go to England. Though he could not come to the States "at all," he could remain with his friends indefinitely. "I got in a bit of debt here and lost passports but all this can be cleared up with a little organization." The only solution lay in my return.

Meantime, and none too soon, Arthur Lowry engaged the legal firm of Basham and Ringe in Mexico City to look after Malcolm's interests. From them I received a detailed letter on June 3. They had discharged Malcolm's debts and re-established him in the capital, but since that climate was "extremely prejudicial to any drinking," they felt it best that he rejoin me. The tone, though gentle, was clear.

I answered at some length. Malcolm and I had been apart for six long months, and his alcoholism had raged on unabated. The impasse that had separated us remained. Only in letters could I talk to him, so on June 11 I again wrote.

"My dearest: It is now one A.M. and for an hour I have been twenty-seven. One year ago, Conrad and Mary were with us. You and I had quarreled. I left for Mexico City, and then Michoacan, where I found your letters and my heart sang. And after Conrad, we did know months of peace, but just a few short months before we were again pursued by furies.

"Those few months remain representative of all the joy we found in one another. We blundered on, hoping time could effect the needed changes, but some problems lie so deep no hopeful tenderness can root them out—only skilled treatment and determination to cooperate."

I then went on to discuss the Menninger's theories and urge Malcolm to consider entering his clinic. "No use to keep assuring me 'I am drinking less and working hard.' You have used this phrase repeatedly to your father. Now you are using it to me. You can be among the finest writers of our time, but as things stand now, today, you seem sadly bent on self-destruction. It is devastating to watch and it destroys us both."

The letter remained unanswered.

Menninger's chapter on alcoholism in *Man Against Himself* was a case history of Malcolm: the father seeking to impose his will; the terrors and hallucination; the flight from opportunities and obligations; attempts to arouse pity through disasters "not of my own doing"; the infantilism and eternal accusations; the need to dominate and yet be cherished; the truculence when drunk; the incessant importunacy. On and on went the similarities.

On Malc's behalf, I wrote to Menninger's and received a helpful two- page response, which offered to send a letter I could forward to Arthur Osborne Lowry, an offer I accepted.

In July I wrote to Malcolm twice, the second time in remembrance of his twenty-ninth birthday. "Did you get my long letter with its suggestions about a clinic, either Menninger's or one comparable? Do write. God bless you and may the O.C. guard and shield you. I send you my love."

On July 28 I made long notes in my journal:

Just returned from seeing *Mayerling* with George and Boske [Antheil]. It is nearly a year since I saw it in Mexico with Malcolm. And today he is 29. Where is he? With whom? I can't think too far in this direction for I picture nothing but the ominous. Certainly I have not gone far if to forget him was what I sought; not a day has passed undominated by memories: our happy months at the Somerset; our renaissance in Mexico after Alan left; and once again when Conrad moved along; although Malcolm was then ill, often in bed while I looked after him. But solitude, invalidism, these are fragile bases though even so I then felt most complete . . . the closest I have ever come to oneness.

Here, I feel half a creature.

In the movies I thought again of Malcolm, recalling Mexico, the little *teatro* where we first saw *Mayerling,* the walk home through the cool streets to the Hotel Canada, bed in each other's arms, the sweetness of taking one another, and my throat closed.

If I might have one prayer, it would be for Malc to place himself in the hands of Menninger and be restored to build again, with me, a life of peace and tolerance. For in every way but one he has given me more than any man I have ever known, knowledge, understanding, depths . . . In every way but one I have loved him most deeply, needed and wanted him most desperately. In every way but one . . .

The next day he showed up.

I had just put Jezebel out for her restricted sunbath on my tiny patio, her furry little body encased in its small harness, attached to a nearby bush by means of a four-foot leash. My minuscule house squatted at the foot of a long gravel drive. There was a larger house, likewise tenanted, in front, separated from my own by a high ivy-covered trellis. I lay near Jez on a canvas beach chair, reading, when I heard the crunch of gravel. And there was Malcolm!

He presented a most alarming figure, drunk, semicoherent, his face marked where, he asserted, he'd been beaten up and robbed by the police. His physical condition appeared deplorable; his nerves shot. He did not remotely resemble the reassuring picture painted by the Mexico City solicitors . . . He resembled the Malcolm I had known in Cuernavaca who had used a towel as pulley for his glass, and my immediate reaction was despairing: we were worse off than ever!

Doubly convinced now that our sole hope lay with Menninger, I cabled Arthur Lowry, who arranged instead for a local attorney by the name of Benjamin Parks. During the many talks I had with this man in the weeks ahead, I found him solely concerned with disposing of Malcolm as expeditiously as possible: in his own words, he did not "have time to play wet-nurse to a drunkard." Anything truly concerned with Malcolm's ultimate good was furthest from his aims, which were merely to sober up a trying charge with the minimum of delay by installing him in a facility "for drunks." He brushed aside any suggestions of psychoanalysis with the comment that such institutions were only run for profit. Dismissing alike Menninger, the New York State Psychiatric Institute, and the clinic of Dr. Austin Riggs in Stockbridge, Massachusetts, he produced instead just such an institution as he'd originally suggested. Appalled, I countered with the proposal that he permit examinations of Malcolm by a trio of specialists: an internist, a neurologist, and a psychoanalyst. Their findings and diagnoses could be forwarded to Arthur Lowry after receiving his permission to proceed. Menninger's provided me with the name of a psychiatrist, and I interviewed him and the other specialists, who concurred on the futility of a band-aid approach.

In spite of all this and his promise to me, Parks undertook to send Malcolm to nothing more than yet another drying-out clinic. None of the specialists was ever called; there were to be no examinations; Parks proceeded to dispose of the case with the least possible inconvenience to himself. By this time, needless to say, we had developed a mutual loathing. And so, in September 1938, Malcolm entered a sanatorium in La Crescenta, and from there Malcolm sent one of the last and longest of his love letters:

Eurydice, my wife, Jan—

Perhaps I am a contradictory Orpheus to be thinking of the songs
you used to charm me with, but that's what I am doing . . . Do you
remember "I am small and slim and my very whim is worthy of a
tippet mouse; I am the mistress of this house, tiddledee, tiddledee,
tiddledee, tiddledee" Please, please, never lose this adorable side of
your nature.

. . . and my God I've been unfair to you and blind, and I curse
myself for all the hard things I've said: call them insults flung at my
own misery. And all the anxiety and suffering, but that is looking
toward the past and we have to look at the future.

. . . oh gosh, those songs of yours: do you remember "I am a
pusscat, you are a pupdog, we are a fam-i-leee, we will go sailing, we
will go bailing over a bright blue sea . . ."

He was thirsting for poetry and books, having only "an enormous and
disastrously dull lexicon of vaguely arctic origin, in which a grim slavey
with wattles takes 887 ½ ill-translated pages to have, by an Eskimo in a
snowdrift, an infant that apparently turns out an idiot in Vol.2, which,
thank God, I haven't got; (two), a book of Spanish poems, *El Cancion,*
of which I can understand just enough to ascertain they are of an
unvintageable lousiness: ex: 'Besare con acentos melodiosos nuestro
enseno de amor, perla divina,' etc.;(three), an exciting yarn by Jack
London I have now read three times, *The Mutiny on the Elsinor,* but so
fouly, oh my perla divina, written, it's beginning to affect my metabo-
lism, also my style, if any. Sunsets are the London special."

Could I arrange to send him books, along with something which
would reassure him of my love; the only things he really craved were
me and poetry . . . and, he added, "well, maybe just one, perhaps, no?"

He had salvaged the damaged *Under the Volcano,* which now
needed to be typed, and finished a story called "Dying, Egypt, Dying,"
still too illegible for typing and possibly needing a different title.

Now at the Sanatorium three weeks, he felt "at ease among the
damned" . . . but the loss of *In Ballast* together with its notes (sent

registered and insured from Mexico) "makes for gaiety in the long loveless hours . . . This of course you wrote down, as all else, to drink . . ."

The place was comfortable, its personnel kindly, and the "routine subtly spaced." But for this and "the sun, larkspurs in the garden, and the possibility of exercise, it would all be Julian Green and Swedenborg with woodcuts out of human hearts by George Grosz."

The other patients were quite without hope, Malc wrote, though unaware of this, their lives "like a dawn they are continually waiting for . . . dawn does not break and the only hope for twilight . . . is the night." Among them were "a famous ex-comedienne, her many times lifted ex-face . . . ghastly and tragic at the same time."

There was a former tycoon whom Malc called Mr. W.; "an anal-erotic who talks of nothing but food;" a woman who made her shoes and hats of toilet paper; a schizophrenic tap-dancer who saw eight million turkeys in the Verdugo Hills . . . "poxily happy;" an old lady who had had a stroke and who could say only "oh baby, wonderful. Absolutely. Misericordia and God help them all."

Did I remember . . . "I've put all my legs in one basket," And by the way, his rheumatism had not been that at all but *infantile paralysis!* A doctor in Mexico had told him the symptoms and "residuals" fitted.

Now he claimed he'd been "imprisoned as a spy because that pimp of a pseudo-communist, Harry, who never got nearer to a war than under his truck at the distant sound of firing on another front and was really thrown out altogether for being useless, had to go about snapping bloody little photographs and shooting off his mouth (which is the only shooting he's ever done like so many of these dreary people) . . . and then afterwards to be interned by my own mind, and dragged back again bleeding from the barbed wire in one after another attempt to escape, to the cell of no word, to bread dry as the heart and water brackish as its blood . . ." Lost without me, he pleaded for some sign I loved him still. Did I remember the last days "before the cataclysm when we were looking at houses around Cuernavaca, and the electric gale up in the hills, and that lonely house with the water rough and cold and blue in the swimming pool, and the cheerless fronton court, the wet grass as we went to see the gardener's newborn child? There was hope, all hope, then . . ."

Did I remember "the owl for all his feathers was a-cold," or "he who keepeth his temper is greater than he who taketh a city?"

How he wished we were boarding the old Fall River boat now; the crackup had been because of his work, "the sense of failure, of not belonging to the world." But "whereas analysis might prove of lasting benefit to my character and to my work, I offer too much of a narcissistic obstruction at the outset for such a process to justify the amount of money entailed to produce what might be simply a wise ratification of what I already know. Besides, there is a good deal of sheer irrationality in my case which is simply not in the books. I do not believe God himself could relieve me of the worm of misery which gnaws at my vitals even when I am happy . . . though I have known pure joy with you . . . surely I could again make you happy, and *us*. Bless you, my own darling, and again and always, bless your heart . . ."

Later he wrote that the disturbing letters I received about him were written at his instigation, that he had felt the news that he was "sinking into a truly frightful state without you might have brought you there to find a house arranged for without the obligations of Cuernavaca, myself sober, good friends, Sherwood Anderson, and a marvelous climate . . . use of both the Rileys' and the Baldwins' yachts . . ."

(There were no yachts in the letters I'd received from Mrs. Baldwin nor those from Malc from Acapulco, from whence it had once again taken his father's attorneys to extricate him. But like the ill-fated MG of 1933, the fantasy of the yachts expanded to assume its own life in memory.)

He wrote that he had now become the pawn in a chess game which has toppled beneath the table: how, then, could he be heard? Though he'd failed to offer reassurance of his love when I'd most needed it ("sometimes the moon comes too near the earth and drives men mad") could I still be generous enough to assure him that I cared? or "ruthless" enough to admit otherwise?

What if he gave up alcohol for two years to "encourage" me? In analysis, though it might "purge my mind of certain distorted and persistent convictions . . . of the roots of human behavior," which, admittedly could only benefit his work "where the worm has her hideout," the cost would be enormous and would "drag my father out by the roots from Liverpool, Conrad from Sussex, Nordahl from Oslo, everything short of clubbing me back into my mother's womb." Should he prove unable to succeed on his own however, he'd then agree analysis offered the final hope.

In closing he asked for the addresses of the *New Republic,* the *New Masses* and *Poetry,* or, failing these, of Peak.

Plainly, he was not to progress beyond the ministrations, however kindly and well-meant, of the sanatorium in La Crescenta. When he left the place, Parks installed him at the Hotel Normandie in Los Angeles.

~ ~ ~

There was never an actual parting, rather a gradual drifting away from one another. We spoke often on the telephone, dined together, and caught movies, but what we were attempting to recapture had grown tenuous. Regardless of his luminous and tender prose, what he sought from me was an unquestioning adherence, drunk or sober, which I could not provide.

For him to promise two years of strict sobriety was tantamount to my vowing an eternal calm. And supposing even the rosiest of outlooks: after two years, what? But the issue presently turned academic as little by little the bars resumed their hold. In this ongoing tug-of-war, our love got lost.

We met for the final time in the summer of 1939. Malcolm seemed odd that day, tense and withdrawn, uncommunicative. Moreover, he looked pale. After we parted, I started worrying that he might be ill and called him at the Hotel Normandie. As he acknowledged me, a female voice shouted across the wire: *"Tell her to go to hell! Tell her to go to hell!"* The note of savagery appalled and startled me . . . not that Malc should be involved in an amour, for under the circumstances that would be understandable, but *this* amour?

If the lady's intention had been to sever us permanently, she achieved her aim. There wasn't a blow up, there wasn't a resolution in which we sat down and confronted each other and said, "Well, this is what we have got to do." There wasn't, as happened to a girlfriend of mine, a situation where the husband came in and said, "Darling, I want a divorce." It drifted. It sifted, like rain falling on a pavement to gradually wash away whatever covered it. We were still tied together and yet the bonds grew more and more elastic, till finally, when I heard that voice on the telephone, it snapped.

Through the mother of a friend, I secured her family attorney and instigated divorce proceedings. In 1939, there were few grounds for divorce, the most innocuous being nonsupport, and that was how I filed. But when I appeared before the elderly crotchet of a judge, he snapped at me. "Well, what did you expect? You left *him,* didn't you?"

I looked at counsel helplessly and waffled. It was then that the attorney changed the grounds to alcoholism, which I had wanted to avoid, and with some grumbling from the bench the interlocutory decree was granted.

An ultimate canard, which found its way into Douglas Day's biography of Malcolm, was that I received a "sizable cash settlement" from Arthur Lowry, through the "good offices" of Mr. Parks. Good offices indeed! I neither sought, expected, nor received this fabled settlement; it would be interesting to speculate upon its disposition. Besides being young, healthy, and fiercely independent, I likewise disapproved of alimony, except in the case of children.

With our divorce now due to finalize late in 1940, only a faltering thread connected us, yet how could we not remain each other's friend? Some part of me would always cherish much that had been dear and memorable, and I saw no reason this could not be mutual. Our parting, after all, had not been acrimonious. And so in April and again in May I wrote Malc in Vancouver, where Parks had taken him at his father's insistence. I wrote not knowing he was there with Margerie Bonner which, point of fact, was no longer any of my business.

Dearest Malc,

We could go on being silent indefinitely on the theory that it would be better to forget all about each other, but why? If there is any hard feeling, it can only have come from outside parties. In our relations it isn't possible there should be anything but affection and respect. I hope this is so, and if it is, I should like always to keep it that way.

There seems no point now in discussing our divorce, but let's not use it as a means of cutting each of us off completely from the other. You were far too important an influence in my life and for a time I think it was mutual. Can we now simply turn our backs on our memories and pretend they never happened?

Perhaps I had better mention at this point that I am not writing because I want anything. I asked for and received nothing, which was as I wished, but I don't know what distorted images Parks may have conjured up to minimize his own financial benefits. You must know me well enough, however, to make your own evaluation. So as I say, I am not writing because I want anything.

As a matter of fact, my circumstances are much the same as when I saw you last. I live at the same place; have acquired a few new clients and so am earning more; have the same literary hopes. It seems that whatever I want I shall earn for myself, which strengthens me. It also sums up and dismisses me.

What about you? What has happened to *Under the Volcano? In Ballast? The Last Address?* And your poetry? Are you still in Vancouver? In love or out? Sending out your work? Do you hear from John? Arthur and Ara? Conrad? John, I understand, left Hollywood owing eight thousand dollars, not bad after only a year and something. He has since, I'm told, come into a lot of money of his own, but no doubt you know all of this already.

There's a lot more I could write, but I'd better first be sure that you may get this and conceivably answer it. Even if you don't answer, I want you to have it because it states my own position and you can know, now, how I feel, and how I wish it to be with us. I can't do anything for you and you can't do anything for me, I imagine, for our problems are probably just as when we last met, but if we can keep our friendship and mutual interest alive and growing, we will have something which will, I hope, become more valuable to us both as time goes on.

Wishing you everything good and fortunate. Jan.

There was no answer, and I read later that Malc had thrown the letter into the fire. I have no copy of my letter of May 20, but in July I wrote to wish him a happy birthday and to enclose a story of mine which had been published in the *Bulletin of the League of American Writers,* entitled "One Goes First." It was my maiden publication and I was proud of it. Having taken a short story class at UCLA Extension in the winter of 1939, I was then studying with Viola Brothers Shore, who was immensely encouraging. (Later still would come a class with Irwin Shaw.)

In planning a trip north with a professor of anthropology whom I was considering marrying when my divorce became final, I thought it might be a pipe of peace to visit Malc while I was in Vancouver and was quite unprepared for the vigor with which he attacked this notion.

"My dear Jan" (his letter of July 27,1940, began:)

Thanks a lot for remembering my birthday and for wishing me luck with my work.

I would of course like to see you, but on cool thinking about this, perhaps it is better not. There is conscription here within the next week, and I am trying hard to complete a job of work before that happens. I have reached a certain stage of peace in the execution of this, from which I have no wish to be interrupted. I am putting this work first, so that I shall not see you. Anyhow, there would be, I feel, too much politeness, too much unexpressed rudeness, too many recollections of forgetfulness, too much of a carefully veiled sense of drama, where no drama is, but only unreality, and finally too much underground bleeding altogether for such a meeting at such a time to have anything more than a nuisance value to either of us. However "sportingly" you may behave now, I shall not be able to help in my heart regarding you as a sort of enemy so long as we remain legally tied. And however hearty I might be, experience teaches me to be wary in advance of your friends, however excellent, and I do not wish to exhibit this conscious wariness even for an afternoon. Your motives are probably good, simple and friendly, but even so I do not wish to see you now. After our divorce, after the war is over, it may, I feel, be different. These two catharses may purge what I hope is at bottom a sincere friendship of its deviousness and treachery. Yet I feel strongly enough about all this, however, to wish that you do not come to Vancouver at all: I should not like to think of you here and not see you. On the other hand I must insist about it; that I do not see you at this time, even if you do come up here. Why here, by the by? It is a deathly dull place and the weather has broken.

Re "One Goes First," I am glad to see you in print, and I think the story has a real quality and a better texture, which sets it above what I have seen of yours. It is an advance of you, I think. A certain value attaches to its publication which may be important to you. I don't know about its sincerity. I think you personally (when you remember) are sincere enough. Yet the point of the story, the "Keep out, keep clear, keep safe, it isn't your affair," part is lifted from *Under the Volcano*. You probably don't remember but there it is: the people going along in the bus, the dying peon, the girl saying to herself it isn't your affair, in the same way . . .

More likely you did remember, but said to yourself: Well, it was a good idea, but Malc was drunk and has lost everything he's written so what the hell? For your own protection I must disabuse you of this illusion. For mine, I say only, and wanly, that I've often worried about how my own work has pirated other people's in the past, and if what work of mine that is to be published in the future is meantime pirated by my ex-wife, I shall find myself in a pretty anonymous position.

Though for all that what you said, what I said, is something that must be said and cannot be repeated too often. Someone does have to go first and I think the fact that I also wrote as much reflects on your way of expressing it.

I hope you may do more and more on your own, and succeed. But you must work harder than you say you do if you are to get anywhere.

There remained little to add, he concluded, except please, if I wrote again, not to put my name on the envelope as Lowry—it would embarrass him with the people in whose hands his affairs were placed to have to admit to having a wife in Los Angeles. So I should continue anonymously and, he hoped, happily. He was, by the way, sorry for me that Paris had fallen to the Germans.

There was an odd thing about this quasi diatribe: for the first time, in all the countless letters he had written me over the years, my name was misspelled on the envelope, and the letter itself was dated, another variant. I answered it at once. As that was his avowedly final letter to me, so would this be, from me to him . . . a woeful ending to our writing-paper love.

Dear Malcolm,

Having just received your letter, let me write at once to assure you of two things: first, since you are so definite about it, I shall on no account look you up in Vancouver, if, in fact, I do go there at all. Secondly, if you will remember, I was likewise on that bus in Mexico and likewise experienced the drama you recall.

However, the scene which you dismiss as "lifted" was actually taken from an incident which befell me in Los Angeles. It was night; I had been covering a meeting of the German-American Bund for the Anti-Nazi League, and I was the girl on the bus with the wounded Negro and the other characters. It was I who reminded myself, "This isn't your affair," etc., not because I was remembering the deathless words in your story, but because it is the natural thing (unfortunately) which one says under such circumstances when trying to avoid responsibility.

It was during a discussion of this episode with Viola Brothers Shore, my instructor, that the story idea developed: if, for instance, the girl had conquered her original timidity and reacted with compassion, would not the tale then find its theme? its idea germ?

I resent such accusations as plagiarism, because I have quite enough to say without having to resort to cribbing so banal a phrase from another. You and I are fundamentally different, as writers, as thinkers, in almost every way. I wish I possessed your genius, and it gives me no pleasure to realize we are unlikely to have further influence upon each other. I have, however, never cast aspersions on our marriage: can you, my darling, say as much to me?

If you will return my "One Goes First" I shall appreciate it. It is my small first-born and I have only one other copy. I admire your impulse to finish a body of work at this perilous time, and know you will be successful. I am deeply sorry to have encountered such bitterness and lack of understanding in your letter, sorry that there cannot be a freer and friendlier bond between us, but I hope in any event you will be happy and successful in whatever you undertake. Jan.

The next time I heard of Malcolm was in 1947 when *Under the Volcano* burst upon the literary scene. It is a monumental work and I am grateful to have been present at its genesis. I would have written him of my delight at the book's emergence, but the thought that he might view my letter (after the years which separated us) as self-serving, even opportunistic, and honed by the memory of his final harsh, accusatory note, dissuaded me.

I could wish that my memories of Malcolm recalled solely the entrancing man I learned to love, and like an averted gaze, might avoid reference to that tormented other who, departing on his implacable visits to the Universal, or the tourist's bar known as the Cadillac, or Charlie's Place, or the Salon Ofelia, would leave me notes assuring me he was "*not doing anything destructive.*" But perhaps, in an ultimate sense, Malcolm was right, for bars are inextricably woven into his legend, and it was they which helped to give him his *Volcano*.

In 1939, when I accepted at last the recognition that our years together must be seen as prelude to what lay ahead, and that any succor analysis might have offered could never come to pass, I realized as well, and finally, that the boat which was Malcolm had slipped its moorings in my life and was putting out to darker seas on which I could not follow. It was a knowledge sad and bitter but quite inescapable.

He was a dazzling man, this Malcolm Lowry. He illumined many lives, produced one masterpiece, and died far too young. We shared a few dreams and a few years and our youth. These were the gifts we gave to one another.

INDEX